Wild Garlic: Quarante, France
Peter Matthews

HOT SUN
COOL SHADOW

Savouring the food, history, and mystery
of the Languedoc

ANGELA MURRILLS

Illustrations by Peter Matthews

Guilford, Connecticut

Edited by Scott Steedman
Design and typesetting by Teresa Bubela

Library of Congress Cataloging-in-Publication Data

Murrills, Angela
  Hot sun, cool shadow : savouring the food, history and mystery of the
Languedoc / Angela Murrills ; illustrations by Peter Matthews.
    p. cm.
  ISBN 978-0-7627-4747-4
  I. Languedoc (France)—Description and travel. 2. Languedoc
(France)—Social life and customs. 3. Americans—France. I. Title.
  DC611.L292M87 2008
  944'.8—dc22
                                        2007034058

Manufactured in the United States of America
First Globe Pequot Edition/First Printing

10 9 8 7 6 5 4 3 2 1

To Kate

CONTENTS

Prologue

Early January. The year feels as pristine as the first page of a child's exercise book. We're still in a holiday mood. Maybe we'll go to a movie, drop in on friends, invite someone over — "but let's stay home tonight," says Peter, "just the three of us." So we do, and after our nine-year-old daughter Kate is tucked in bed, we talk, not about how long the winter will last but about the year, indeed the years, ahead. Somehow that first page on the calendar always creates a feeling of hope, of being on the brink, of making change. How could we have known at the time that what will emerge from this evening will be years of roaming and discoveries, culminating in a single moment?

I t stood at the periphery of the village on a calm little side street, an *impasse* in French. At its end the street made a dog-leg turn into a yard, which meant we'd be exposed to minimal traffic beyond the egg-yolk yellow *poste* van. The blue-and-white sign at the corner read *"Impasse de l'église"*: we'd be close enough to the church that we could rely on its bells to tell us the time. A stable in its previous incarnation and still a work-in-progress, the house was one in a row of small modest cottages. Framed by the living room window, a west-facing garden over-looked nothing but lawns, cherry trees, the side of an old barn and the green mounds of hills in the far distance; the view was even better from the balcony upstairs off the main bedroom. The stone wall in the *salon* had already been uncovered, and for the mantel there was a length of oak, found in a former shed, that was so ancient you could pass your hand along it and feel the faint indentations where generations of horses had rubbed it with their chins. Outdoors there would be a terrace and a built-in fireplace to grill *merguez* (spicy lamb sausages) and *magrets de canard* (duck breasts), with space to plant thyme and rosemary right next to it.

We'd been coming to the Languedoc for eight years by then, loving the region more with each visit. Even if we did not yet have a French house of our own (the search for one, if never full-time, was ongoing), we were already putting down roots of a minor kind: buying an elderly, diesel-fuelled war-horse to save on car rental costs and parking it in a barn when we went away; signing up for a *carte de fidélité* at the local Champion supermarket; and, this time, leaving two boxes behind in our friend Nigel's attic. Inside them were four yellow-checked napkins, a towel, a cake of lavender soap, salt from the Camargue, coarse-grained mustard, wine vinegar, three bottles of local Fitou wine and a bottle of pastis still half full: we viewed them as a start, a commitment, tangible evidence that we would be back. One afternoon towards the end of our stay we were sitting outside in the sun, looking across at the great surging shape of the mountain of Montségur, having a cup of tea with Nigel — who wakes up to this view every morning — and telling him about our latest house-hunting failures. Too large, too close to the trucks thundering by, a roof that sagged like an old mattress. A pleasant enough cottage but the village had no *boulangerie*, a serious lack if your daydreams include pre-breakfast saunters down the street for fresh croissants.

Why don't you check out the house that belongs to ___ ?, and Nigel named a couple we had met on a previous visit. It's small, he said. That was fine. It's in ___ , and he mentioned a village we not only knew and liked but had actually stayed in some years earlier. They're renovating, he said (better and better), and I think they might want to sell. So we went and looked.

To be blunt, it was a mess, as house renovations invariably are. Standing there amid the clutter and the stacks of lumber, we tried to imagine the finished structure as the owners explained their intention to use materials and architectural details salvaged from this house and others; *récupérer* is the French word. We saw additions when we dropped in a few days later, a turn-of-the-century glass-panelled door with Gothic arches, an old beam exposed over the kitchen window, the wide-planked floor upstairs. En route to Toulouse the day before we headed back to North America, we paid one last visit to a place we already felt at home in.

"But won't it be too small?" said Peter, somewhere over the Rockies.

At around five metres wide and perhaps twice that in length, it was inarguably a compact house but, going over the plans with the owners, I had come to admire how well every square centimetre would be utilized. I reminded him of the spacious pantry, the little cupboard just the right size for bottles of gas for the stove. "And there's all that space under the stairs. In England," I continued, exaggerating only slightly, "people often convert that space into a second bathroom."

"I'll need a studio to paint in."

"How about the front room upstairs?"

"What about when people come to stay?"

"We could section off half the space with folding doors. That way, they'd have a view of the château."

Its turret and battlements, glimpsed across the treetops of a neighbour's garden, were just one more draw.

"We're interested," we wrote in a letter to France some days later. Phone calls followed, and photos and floor plans with measurements, so that, even from far away, we could start planning where to position paintings and bookshelves. And, most important of all, the dining table.

In the end, it was as simple as that.

What we couldn't have realized during that first visit to the chaotic building site was how ideally the house was positioned. How the morning light would filter through the lace curtains in the kitchen, casting muzzy wavering shadows on the tiled floor, and how, by early afternoon, the earth would tilt enough to send sunlight flooding in through the living room window (exceptionally large for a French cottage, it had once been the *vitrine* of a shop).

We knew the provenance of just about everything in the house. That was the bonus of buying a place that was still in the works — and not yet complete when we returned to France almost a year later to finalize the formalities. Realizing that more hands would help us to move in sooner, we rolled up our sleeves and joined a crew that seemed to change daily; at least thirty people contributed to the labour of love. Philippe, the master carpenter who built the kitchen cupboards, was a man so enamoured of wood that he once came out into the garden where we were planting herbs bearing a handful of fresh curly shavings, just so we could share his pleasure in their resinous tang. In between sharing recipes Bernard, another carpenter, never tired of telling us why he had left his job in a Manhattan restaurant to return to his native France.

Whether we were grouting the tiles on the kitchen counters or brushing coats of varnish onto the wooden floors upstairs, we always made time for lunch. Shortly before midday, a sheet of plywood was lugged into the garden and set on a couple of trestles. On it went a bottle of local *rouge*, a wedge or two of cheese, some earthy *pâté de campagne*, a metre of baguette and a salad. The angelus bell at noon was the signal to down tools.

"Remember how this whole adventure started?" I said to Peter some ten days later as he popped the cork on a bottle of Blanquette to celebrate that we were finally in. The same bells had pealed at the precise moment we were unlocking the front door for the first time as the house's official new owners. I feel sure now that it was the same kind of coincidence, synchronicity, divine providence, call it what you will, that brought us here in the first place.

I CAN'T RECALL what we did on that January evening in Canada all those years earlier but, typically, I can tell you exactly what we ate. With the last of the Christmas bird gone to soup in the freezer, I had roasted a chicken (massaged first with olive oil and garlic), tossed a watercress salad and set out a loaf of rough-crusted bread: our kind of food, simple and straightforward, especially with a lusty Merlot to go with it. Much later, with Kate in bed but wine left in the bottle, Peter and I began talking about the future, specifically about finding another place we could eventually call home for part of the year. I am a journalist, he was then a full-time art director, and our "commute" was a thirty-second walk down to our basement office. Even so, we still found ourselves far too busy most of the time. City stress was getting to us; much of the consumer-based North American way of life made less and less sense. We yearned for a simpler life in rural surroundings where we could write, paint and cook to our hearts' content. I might even take up that guitar I hadn't touched in twenty years. It was a long-term plan. We were still very much involved in our careers. More to the point, Kate was still only nine years old. But she had two passports — one European, courtesy of my British upbringing — and when she grew up, we wanted her to feel comfortable in two cultures.

Individually and collectively, where would we all feel at home? Cornwall, Dublin ("Writers don't pay income tax in Ireland") and Tuscany all came up for discussion but were discarded for reasons to do variously with living costs, weather and an inability to speak Italian. In hindsight, the decision was staring us in the face.

It had to be a place where food played the leading role, where food ruled.

From farm or orchard to table, the entire continuum fascinates us, especially when it results in uncomplicated dishes made with local ingredients. As a journalist, I was hot on the topic of eating regionally and seasonally, and not only for environmental reasons: tomatoes in July just tasted better. Food has always driven us. Our first stop in any city or town is always its market; in fact, at Kate's naming ceremony when she was five months old, we went on record promising that we would take her to markets whenever we could. The cookbook collection had invaded every room in a house which smelled more often of sizzling onions than of potpourri; even in mid-winter, I don rubber boots to go out to the garden to snip fresh parsley or forage for chickweed. We live to eat, not the opposite. Where else could we logically end up but France?

Agreed. "Now we just have to decide where," said Peter.

Pinpointing a specific region was less straightforward. France is a colossal five-pointed star, its northern shore visible on a cloudless day from the chalky cliffs of England, its closest southern landfall the African coast. In cinematic terms, we needed to zoom in from an aerial shot to a medium close-up. I pulled our *National Geographic Atlas of the World* off the bookshelf, opened it to France and reached for a pencil. Normandy? Brittany?

"Too rainy," said Peter. "Remember, that's why we don't want to go to England. We can get rain *here*."

The great platform of the Massif Central? Too remote. Logically, the pencil slid south towards the Côte d'Azur (too crowded), bypassed Provence (too well-known) and crossed the Rhône, slowing down and halting slightly south and east of Toulouse at a city called Carcassonne.

I circled it.

It was a Proust's madeleine of a name for both of us. Carcassonne. A mass of images and sounds crowded in: medieval stone walls topped with towers and battlements, pennants slapping in the wind, the thud of hooves and clinking of armour across a drawbridge. But beyond Carcassonne's reputation as the most perfectly preserved walled city in Europe, we knew embarrassingly little about it or the region it stood in, the Languedoc. Geographically the area looked promising, with the Mediterranean coast and the Pyrenees both close by. Gastronomically, I knew of the legendary rustic dish called *cassoulet* and had heard rumbles of increasingly creditable wines.

"Collioure." Peter pointed to a town near the Spanish border. "That's where Dufy and Matisse painted." He tapped the page higher up. "And I think there's a terrific Toulouse-Lautrec museum in Albi." The region's shadowy art and food connections had tweaked our imaginations but by now it was well past midnight, the wine bottle was empty and the fire had died. More concrete plans could wait till tomorrow. We would sleep on it.

Woken abruptly at eight the next morning, I shrugged on a dressing-gown and stumbled dozily out to the landing to answer the phone. "You don't know me," said an unfamiliar male voice, "my name's Robert." And he went on to explain that he was in

Vancouver on business and needed to contact a knitwear designer I had written about for a magazine.

"Where do you normally live?"

"In the south of France," the mysterious Robert replied. "You won't have heard of the village. It's called Chalabre and it's about half an hour south of Carcassonne."

Knees really do turn to water. I fetched the information he wanted in a hurry, then got into serious conversation, words tumbling over themselves.

"What size is your village? What's it like?"

"Who is it?" Peter called sleepily from the bedroom.

"Can we all get together soon?" I said into the phone.

Within weeks, a glass of wine at a downtown tapas bar had evolved into friendship, dinners and an invitation to visit if we were ever in the area.

Not if, we said, when.

Four months later found us speeding towards Toulouse on a sleek TGV (*train à grande vitesse*) that knifed through the landscape too fast to leave much beyond a blurred impression of the countryside. We had decided not to take Kate out of school for this exploratory visit; settled in with relatives, she was perfectly happy as long as we brought back the promised stack of horse magazines. As the train slid south we could see the topography changing, the flat land rucking up into rolling hills dotted with cows. Like pistachio ice cream sprinkled with chocolate, I thought, my mind as usual on edible matters and the lunch that had been the high point of the seven-hour journey from Paris. At some unspoken signal, everyone in the carriage unpacked their provisions. The two *grandmères* across from us brought out cloth napkins, slices of bread and *charcuterie* wrapped in waxed paper.

The old man in the corner unsnapped a small leather suitcase as brown and creased as his face, rooted around among his garments and produced a sausage and a knife. Now it was our turn. Kept overnight in a warm Paris hotel room, the Camembert we had bought the previous day had attained its summit of odorous ripeness and was now sliding fast down the other side, releasing pungent locker-room exhalations as I unleashed it from its plastic bag. Eyes watered, delicate coughs were produced, but nobody complained and, as each person left the carriage, they wished us *bonne continuation* — enjoy the rest of your journey. We liked the people around here already. They had a decent respect for the palate.

Outside the Gare Matabiau, Toulouse's palatial railway station, Robert was waiting to meet us. We shoehorned ourselves and our luggage into his car and left the city, branching off a violently busy multi-lane highway to join a two-lane road across rolling countryside. "The further we get from Toulouse," Robert pointed out, "the more you'll feel as though you're going back through history." He was right about that. Somnolent this late in the day, the villages we passed through seemed timeless, the pale facades of their houses like enigmatic faces, eyes shuttered, mouths closed. The sky darkened and raindrops began to fall, bouncing off the road as we drove through a thunderous twilight. Lightning split the sky like silver stitching on velvet and a sudden flash of purple turned ruins on a hilltop into an inky silhouette. Through the fan-shaped spaces cleared by the windscreen wipers, we made out the dim outline of a bell tower. "It's like going back through the decades," said Robert. "You start in the last part of the twentieth century, then go through the '70s, the '60s, the '50s ..." Scrolling back through the years.

Chalabre lay cupped in a valley, the spire of its church protruding from a tumble of red-ribbed roofs. Like any self-respecting village in southern Europe, it had a pizzeria and a café or two, and areas set aside for a market and *boules* games. With its half-timbered houses and its central square accessed by narrow streets, it was a typically attractive Languedocien community; except that, somewhere back in time, the villagers must have decided that if one was good, two were better. To the two small rivers that trickle through Chalabre they added two main streets lined with plane trees and two châteaux, one a colossal structure high on the hill looming over the village, the other the Victorian *petit château* where Robert lived.

Over the next week, as Robert drove us around, we grew more and more beguiled by the region. Our initial attraction was fast developing into a fully blown affair. The unexpected variety and sheer beauty of the scenery made it hard to believe that this land had only merited slivers of chapters in guidebooks even a decade ago. We were just getting used to the morning routine of buying croissants from the *boulangerie* and could hardly bear to leave, but guests can only stay so long in good conscience. After ten days we waved "au revoir" from our rented Renault and returned reluctantly to Paris for the flight home. Even then we realized that fate had brought us to a place that would become central to our lives.

Putting a passion into words, explaining why you are smitten with anything — a person, a job, a country — is never easy. But in the case of the Languedoc, the land speaks for itself. The appeals of its thyme-scented *garrigue* (the rough scrub that covers the inland hills), idyllic pastureland and sun-baked valleys are self-evident, but it's the abrupt flashes in temperament that delight us, the distant mountain crags that suddenly encroach on a serene valley, the fertile plains that give way to flawless beaches, the eerie flat landscape of the Camargue and the coastal lagoons known as *étangs*.

"For me, it's the colours," said Peter, viewing the ochres and russets and blues with an artist's eye.

"Did you know they were once one of the Languedoc's chief industries?" By then, I had read every guidebook I could get my hands on. Pigments were mined in Roussillon, the area that was once a separate kingdom but is now the southwestern part of the region; it is named after the red soil. Toulouse was so renowned for the plant-based blue dye called woad — *pastel* in French — that the area south of it, enriched by this trade, became known as the Land of Cockagne, after the small balls or *coqanes* of the dried leaves. Even today the name suggests a place of milk and honey.

Oh, those intense southern colours. In the interminable grey dreariness of a Pacific Northwest winter, I would close my eyes and revisit the cities of pink-red brick, the bottle green ribbon of the Canal du Midi, the village houses with walls a colour midway between honey and ash. I would picture the candles of purple wisteria and swags of scarlet roses strung across the tops of windows and the shutters faded to soft pinks and blues by the harsh summer sun. I still kick myself for not having my camera with me the day I turned a corner and saw a washing line of faded blue jeans and overalls against vivid green leaves and a stormy indigo sky, with a border of drenched purple irises in the foreground.

But for all its physical charms and startling diversity, the Languedoc has stayed in the shadows for centuries. In the years following our first visits, we become adept at drawing little maps to show friends where its boundaries fell. And they weren't alone in their lack of knowledge: in his *ABC of French Food*, British author Len Deighton calls the Languedoc "a region where the cooking is hearty and delicious, its history and folklore long and colourful. Unfortunately no one seems to know exactly where it is." In 1955, in a bizarre teaming of rock and sunshine, the French government created the *département* (region) of Languedoc–Roussillon, a broad arc that stretches east to the Rhône and southwest to where France meets Spain at the southern coast. (While part of the medieval Languedoc, certain places described in the following pages fall outside today's official borders.) "It's all of France in one place," a woman at the

Carcassonne tourist office told us. This is especially true of the region's mix of history and modernity; human bones unearthed here thirty years ago were shown to be the oldest ever found in Europe, yet less than twenty kilometres from the archaeological site are purpose-built seaside resorts.

While still a massive region, the Languedoc is small compared to its former grandeur, when the court of Toulouse matched the court of Paris in splendour. North and south spoke different dialects adapted from the Latin that was part of the legacy of the Romans. While northerners used the word "oïl" — which evolved into "oui" — for "yes," the southerners said "oc." The language of "oc" — *langue d'oc* in French — was a broad brushstroke that tinted all of southern France, a musical tongue somewhere between French and Spanish and very close to Catalan. This beautiful liquid language, the rolling, sonorous tongue of the troubadours, swirled away into the mist, swept under by the religious wars of the eleventh and twelfth centuries while the language of "oïl" developed into present-day French. Virtually dead for almost seven hundred years, the language of "oc" was revived in the mid-nineteenth century by a Provençal poet, Frédéric Mistral. Today it is taught in southern universities, books are published in *occitan* and at least one primary school we know of has a bilingual program.

The brutal wars that destroyed the everyday speech of the Languedoc were aimed at annihilating Catharism, a Christian "heresy," based partly on Eastern European beliefs, that had grabbed hold of the imagination in southern France to the point where the Church of Rome perceived it as a real threat. From a modern vantage point, the Cathars don't seem that dangerous. They believed in Christ but thought that while God had created the soul, the Devil had created the world — and the body.

The Cathars' faith was a quest for the perfection and purity that would gain them access to heaven; hell was here on earth. It was a strict religion that followed the rules set down in the Bible — to a Cathar, for instance, "thou shalt not kill" meant a vegetarian diet — but did not include Holy Communion. To the Cathars, body and blood were the work of the devil.

The Church hierarchy decided that the heresy must be stamped out before it spread any further and when preaching didn't work, they switched to violence. A great army from the

Laroque Volmes 13th Century Church

north, a tide of iron leaving unspeakable slaughter in its wake, swept down through the Languedoc, pillaging, killing and torturing. The only defence that the Cathars had was their faith — and their castles, a series of mighty mountaintop fortresses whose ruins still stand like massive chess pieces, defenders of valleys and plains, defenders of a sect that is no more than a memory today. It took more than a century and many thousands of lives, but Catharism was suppressed and the lands of Oc became part of France.

To us, the difference between "oc" and "oïl" seemed to typify the difference between north and south. Try saying them aloud. "Oïl" is smooth agreement. "Oc" is an honest down-to-earth bark that reflects the sturdy independence of the people. Far from Paris and, unlike other regions of southern France, rarely considered "fashionable," the Languedoc has been slow to change, and even though technology and improved transportation are making it more accessible, the region is still highly individual. Especially in what goes on its tables.

Right across France, everyday cooking has always been the offspring of land and weather, and the dishes in a Languedoc *livre de cuisine* (cookbook) are no exception. The makeup of its terrain, its turbulent rivers, long Mediterranean coastline, arid hill soil and rolling pasture, are all clues that fish, meat and herbs play important roles. It's a cuisine that isn't urbanely refined but unfussy and rustic, taking the swiftest possible route from barn or brook to table. As anywhere else in rural France, the form of the Languedoc day is shaped by the needs of the stomach; breakfast is not something you linger over but lunch is two hours at a minimum, often three. On our first visit we got caught time and again, plans for a picnic cancelled when the church clock's tinny striking of noon synchronized with the unambiguous shutting of the *boulangerie* door. By default, we became experts in uncomplicated sandwiches of baguette, butter and ruby-coloured country ham and croque-monsieurs, the French variation on grilled cheese sandwiches that are all most small cafés offer. Now we are wiser. We breakfast early and lightly so that by noon we are ready to sit down for a proper meal under the plane trees.

Even to the less food-obsessed, picturing the entire region as a buffet table isn't difficult. At times I'm tempted to view a map of the Languedoc in the same way that the sixteenth-century painter Arcimboldo interpreted the human face: as an intricate collage of fruits and vegetables. The red roads that mark major highways swell up into veins pulsing with robust Merlot and Fitou; the yellow country byways are the duck and goose fat that cushions farm-packed foie gras; the browns of the mountains are reminders of sausages and confit; the lush greens of the meadows are salads. The whole region is one colossal pantry.

Except, of course, that it's far more than that. To Peter and me the Languedoc has become a second home and this book recounts our deepening *affaire de coeur* with it. Ever since that first trip in 1993 — and we have spent increasing numbers of months in France every year, exploring it as a family, a couple or occasionally on our own — the Languedoc has never failed to beguile us.

From our initial reconnaissance trip we knew we wanted to own a house here, to be able to go to the *boulangerie* first thing each morning and buy *pains aux raisins* or baguettes from the people who baked them. While we had begun noticing *À vendre* signs tacked to shutters, we had been too busy to consult a real estate agent and had no idea what property cost. Then, on our last day in Chalabre, our host, Robert, indicated an empty place for sale beside the river. We finagled the key from a neighbour and took a look inside. Granted, there were visible holes in the stone walls and suspicious brown stains suggestive of damp on the faded flowered wallpaper, but the banister was a single sinuous curve of wood polished by generations of hands, the bedrooms were warmed by marble fireplaces and the asking price was

half the cost of the tiniest flat in the city we came from. The house had a *grenier* too, which we later learned meant an attic, with a Vélux, the popular term for a skylight. We were sold, and so, it turned out, was this particular dwelling. But the seed had been planted; the dream was a possibility.

It was to take us seven years to realize it.

CHAPTER 1

Confit de Canard

ALBI, CASTRES AND CARCASSONNE

On the shelf over the sink is my collection of old tins, some chipped, most faded, that once held chicorée or rice. Next to them is a stack of Cuisine Actuelle, the food magazine I buy every month. Recipes beat blockbuster novels any time, even in a language that isn't your own. Delving into cassoulet, the core dish of the Languedoc, had introduced us to a whole new vocabulary, one of couennes, cocos de Pamiers and, above all, confit — preserved duck and goose. We ate confit with gusto on every visit and I pined for it when I wasn't in France. "Next time we go," I said to Peter, "let's try to find out how it's made."

T aking the road out of Carcassonne north towards the Black Mountains, we veered off shortly before the city of Albi onto a side road that eventually led to a farm. No, we weren't here for the bed and breakfast; what we were curious about, I explained to the jovial man who answered the door, were the dishes produced (in fact raised) on his farm, especially confit of duck, for which there seemed to be a thousand recipes. Come in, talk to my wife. Within minutes, Madame Renée Rolland had sat us down in her kitchen, poured us coffee and begun to set us straight.

Her elbow firmly planted on the round wooden table, one hand cupping her chin as the other tapped confidently at the recipe, she was adamant: to make confit correctly, you must add the salt thirty minutes before you finish cooking the duck. *"Non,"* said her son Alexandre, who had just walked into the room. You must salt the duck for *ten hours* before it goes on the stove. Discussion was frenzied. I was not about to take sides, but they were both correct. Making confit is like roasting beef or baking bread — provided it works, your own way is indisputably the right one. That the Rollands, *mère et fils,* crossed amiable swords over technique wasn't surprising. When to salt, whether to add herbs, how long to cook it and how many weeks to let it ripen in its stone jar: ways of making confit are as numerous as the generations of Languedociens who have rolled up their sleeves and got to work on the year's batch as winter approaches. What everyone in the region does agree on is that, both on its own and as an ingredient in other dishes, unctuous confit with its forthright flavour and delectable richness is one of the wellsprings of Languedoc cuisine.

Duck or goose simmered leisurely in its own fat might not sound appealing to appetites outside France, but culinary alchemy happens when maize-fattened poultry is rubbed with salt and seasonings (or not, depending on who you consult), left overnight, slowly simmered the following day and then left to mature like fine wine. While methods differ from household to household, the preparatory steps are always the same.

Madame Rolland grabbed a used envelope from the stack of opened mail on the table and Peter started to pay closer attention as she sketched the outline of a duck — or, rather, a dead duck. A few more strokes of her pencil and off came legs, wings, *magrets* (the steak-sized breasts) and neck. Singly or in combination, the Rollands make all of these into the *confit de canard* that they sell at their farm, La Ferme de Rayssaguel, and at Albi's weekly market.

"What about the duck's head?" I said. Very little is discarded in the Languedoc kitchen.

Madame Rolland gave a dismissive wave at the mere notion of *confit de tête de canard.*

"The head? It goes in the *poubelle.*"

The rubbish bin. Right. Of course.

This is a rare example of waste in a lexicon of cooking that evolved from the needs of hard-working people living in drafty stone farmhouses. Confit is both edible defence and psychological ballast against bone-chilling winters, an age-old method of preserving duck, geese and other meats. Central heating and other forms of progress mean there's no real need these days for the autumnal shift to food designed for interior warmth: we can now eat salads year-round. But what a sense of security a Languedocienne farmwife must have felt in earlier centuries, aware that her pantry shelves groaned with tall brown pottery jars of confit ready to nourish her family all through the bitter winter. No etymological justification exists, but it seems more than coincidence that *confort* — the French word for comfort — and *confit* sound so alike.

In the Languedoc, confit implies duck or goose and while the wings, breasts or necks can all be utilized, the term in general refers to the leg. The word itself simply means "preserved" and, like many French culinary mainstays, its invention probably evolved from frugality. Even in Roman times (and some say earlier), farmers knew that when you fed a duck to the bursting point, more than its liver enlarged. Remove that desirable *foie gras* — literally, "fat liver" — and you were left with the remains of a severely overweight bird. Cook it in its fat and you had *confit*.

Properly made, confit is edible velvet, rich but in no way greasy. I can eat it any time; in the Languedoc, where it's as ubiquitous as chicken drumsticks are in North America or the U.K., I do. Peter and I buy it from the butcher's truck at outdoor markets, where the "confit-ed" duck legs protrude from a sea of white fat like the masts of a spectral ship. We've picked up the big 1400-gram cans holding four legs apiece that stand on the shelves of the Champion supermarket, and eyed with greed and longing the institutional-size cans that hold three times that amount. We have also re-created confit in Canada with some success, although it took a while to find the duck legs. Less painstaking to make from scratch than it sounds, confit is a fast food to bring to the table once it has been prepared, warmed through in the oven, the grill turned on for the last few minutes to transform the skin to crunchy parchment.

Spending time in France would teach me how a cuisine came into being — there was an appealing logic to it, a rational succession of steps. In fashionable restaurants in France and elsewhere, chefs now paint from the entire palette of spices and seasonings, cook fish flown in from anywhere in the world, have arcane vegetables grown especially for them. But the rustic food of the Languedoc, like peasant fare anywhere, is a simple marriage of need and availability, its canon of recipes handed down by word of mouth. If you have nothing but ducks, cabbage and potatoes to work with, you come up with as many ways to cook them as you can. Confit was a case in point.

If it weren't such a farmhouse dish, you could compare confit to the ubiquitous "little black dress" beloved by all French women; it's that versatile. Depending on the season, Madame Rolland said she served her preserved duck with wild mushrooms, celery or lentils: *"c'est super"* with any of these, she exclaimed. "We make it the way that *we* want to eat it," added her husband Paul, speaking of confit and the other regional dishes — foie gras, pâté and *tripous* (rolls of tripe cooked with vegetables) — that the family produces at their farm. "To have quality in the kitchen," he continued, "you must allow time, be organized and have good ingredients." I have heard the same thoughts from many of North America's most lauded chefs; after a couple of decades of fusion and fancifulness, maybe cooking really is getting back to its roots. But tempting though it was to sit and talk food philosophy with the Rollands, it was now time to say *au revoir* and rejoin the main road that led towards Albi.

I can't imagine living with someone who isn't as nuts about food as I am and, though my drawing skills are still at the doodling stage, I'm as fascinated by art as Peter is. To these common interests we had now added a third: the history of the Languedoc. So once we had parked the car on a side street in

Albi, it was a toss-up which to revisit first: the cathedral or the shrine to Toulouse-Lautrec. Religion only won out because it was closer.

They say that the city is called *Albi le rouge* because of the tint of its bricks, but sometimes we wondered if the name didn't stem from its blood-drenched history. Straddling the river Tarn and dominated by the massive block of its cathedral, the city is central to the epic story of the Cathars. Albi gave its name to the Albigensian crusade, a religious army sent by Pope Innocent III

in 1209 to wipe out the increasingly popular, and therefore dangerous, Cathar sect. By 1244, the movement was virtually destroyed, but the Church of Rome decided it needed a powerful symbol of its clout to show any lingering doubters who was in charge. Begun in 1282 and built over the next two centuries, the Cathedral of Saint Cecile would provide it.

Driving across the countryside towards Albi, you pass through a landscape that looks comfortably familiar, its green tree-lined fields and hilltop villages the stuff of children's storybooks. With its half-timbered houses and streets lined with cafés and boutiques, the old section of Albi is friendly and intimate — which makes your first close-up view of the cathedral all the more shocking. Entering a square on the edge of this amiable neighbourhood we came face-to-face with a solid bastion of roseate bricks that stretched high above us, a building with all the hefty menace of a schoolyard bully. It wasn't our first visit to Albi, but the edifice still startled us with its bulk. If we found these sheer prison-like walls daunting in the twentieth century, how much more threatening they must have seemed to the local farmers, weavers and townspeople in the thirteenth and fourteenth as they watched their new place of worship taking shape, not a delicate hymn in stone like most cathedrals of the time but an ominous red fist. Having proved its might by the sword, the Church of Rome now carried its message through in brick with armour-like buttresses and window slits that seemed better designed to spit arrows than inhale light. Standing at the base of the cathedral, I craned my neck to where uncountable courses of unbroken brick stretched above me, more rampart than wall. The message was clear: this place did not house a benign God but an awesome presence ready to smite anyone who stood against Him.

It's difficult to imagine the sway religion once had over the population in an age when mass is only said once a month in many village churches (including ours) and the *presse*, like news stores everywhere, sells magazines that, in earlier times, would have meant long, sweaty-palmed hours in the confessional. Ironically, holiness and sin are close physical neighbours in Albi, the fearsome hell depicted in the cathedral frescoes right next door to the fleshy heaven painted by the city's most famous son, Toulouse-Lautrec, and displayed in the Palais de la Berbie, which (you can almost hear triumphant demonic laughs at this) was formerly the bishop's palace.

In medieval times, Albi was a significant centre, the heredi- tary home of the counts of Toulouse, whose lands sprawled across southern France. Paradoxically, one sadly stunted sprig of this splendid family tree, Henri de Toulouse-Lautrec, became better known than all his illustrious forefathers, famed today as the chronicler of the *louche* Paris of gaslights and tinsel. As the son of an aristocratic family, Henri could have lived as a pam- pered invalid; as a son of the Languedoc, a yearning for inde- pendence probably ran in his blood. For Henri, that included excursions into the *demi-monde* of moist skin and stained satin, and an honest recording of it.

When he died in 1901 at the age of thirty-six, Toulouse- Lautrec's mother donated the works in his studio to his home- town of Albi and funded a museum in his name. It's a rivetting collection and every time we visit we are moved by the man and his works. It is a chastening experience to track his artistic progres- sion from equine paintings bounding with energy to unvarnished depictions of brothel life (it delighted me that the *real* purple banquette we sat on was an exact replica of one in a painting of cap

Alcohol, absinthe, whatever

glass

glass stopper

cane

morose-looking prostitutes waiting
for clients). Seeing real prints of the familiar dance-hall
posters is like meeting old friends: the swaggering Aristide
Bruant with his broad-brimmed hat, voluminous coat and scarlet
muffler worn like a challenge; the voluptuous La Goulue ("the
glutton," a woman who, rumour had it, could kick a man's hat
off his head) in the arms of café-owner Valentin Le Désossé
(literally "the boneless one," so-called for his rubbery agility on
the dance floor at the Moulin Rouge).

The museum also houses photographs and possessions that
expose the human side of the short man with the beard, thick-
lensed glasses, bowler hat and cane. He needed the cane, we discovered, for more than physical support: its hollow interior was
fitted with a tiny glass designed to hold alcoholic refreshment. A
passionate food-lover who carried a nutmeg and a miniature
grater around with him to flavour his port, Toulouse-Lautrec was
also a keen amateur cook who drew whimsical invitations and
menus for his private soirées. His childhood friend, the gourmet
Maurice Joyant, even published a book of recipes the two had
shared; their recipe for confit of goose advocates adding salt *after*
the meat is cooked. Had Toulouse-Lautrec been able to sit down
with the Rollands, what a lively discussion that would have been.

An hour or two in the company of Toulouse-Lautrec is a
must any time we are in Albi, and his hues and brushstrokes

were still whirling through my mind one balmy June evening the following year as we made our way to the outdoor restaurant at the Hôtel Lapérouse. Luxuriant, almost overgrown, the ivy-walled garden blazed with orange blossoms and roses. I tried to view the surroundings with an artist's eye, noting the faded hydrangea-printed napkins, orchid-pink placemats and ribbed glasses on our umbrella-shaded table. At the next table, a couple (vintage 1945 or thereabouts, an excellent year) seemed to epitomize French chic, her hair, pearls and sweater the colour of moonlight, his casual wear a study in charcoal. Toulouse-Lautrec and his sketchpad would have had a field day.

Peter did too. Me, I was into the food, which seemed all of a piece with those slyly erotic paintings. With what seemed like *fin de siècle* abandon, the confit of chicken shrugged off its meat at the touch of a fork, eager to get closer to the fried potatoes, melting leeks and crisp green beans, a naughty, sensual plateful. The salad we ate beforehand is a regional favourite, a mix of curly frisée, Roquefort, walnuts and croutons with a mustardy vinaigrette. Albi was hosting a jazz festival that week and around us, like saxophones passing a musical theme to clarinets, musicians segued fluidly between English and French. As we left, slowly climbing the stairs from the restaurant to the street, we looked down at the now darkened garden, its multicoloured lights, red, yellow, blue and white, strung like necklaces, and the roses that clambered two storeys high, sensual reminders of Paris gas-lamps and boudoir perfumes that accompanied us into the night.

The Toulouse-Lautrec museum had been in our plans as soon as we knew we would be visiting the Languedoc: it was like Notre Dame and Paris or the Colosseum and Rome. But leaving Albi the morning after our first visit, we were unaware of the

delights of a town called Castres some forty kilometres south,
and almost bypassed it. Travelling loosely, rather than with a
tightly scheduled itinerary, frees you to make discoveries, to
journey on whim, to stay overnight if a place turns out to have
promise. The day was hot, with foamy clouds like meringue
shells gliding across the sky. We were going to drive right
through Castres, if it wasn't for the serendipitous combination of
a handy parking space and an inviting back street. We followed
it and came upon a small-scale Venice: tall, ancient houses in
muted pastel colours lining a river, their images upside-down
in the calm water, an arched stone bridge and its reflection
creating a perfect oval.

One thing you notice exploring any part of the country is
that French urban planners appear to draw from a limited bank
of names. Almost every town has a boulevard Victor Hugo, a rue

Voltaire and, in the Languedoc, a street or avenue that commemorates the scholar and politician Jean Jaurès. Albi has a large square named in his memory and Castres, where he was born in 1859, has both a museum and a square with a statue of him at one end. This long, shaded *place* is the site of a lively thrice-weekly market where the spitted chickens slowly revolve in the rotisserie truck, dripping their juices onto a steel trough packed with chopped potatoes, onions and tomatoes. The smell, if you haven't eaten for a while, is enough to drive you mad. But on that first visit, I managed to keep temptation at bay: we had already earmarked a side-street bistro for supper.

Inside La Madragore, modern paintings — startling photorealistic images of everyday objects such as thumbtacks — stood boldly against the grey stone walls. On the table, the treatment of confit was another one to add to the ideas file. Its leg encircled with a paper frill (I thought irreverently of a can-can dancer's knickers), the duck came with spinach, a grilled half-apple, a cake of potato and a heady dollop of garlic-infused tomato coulis: more proof that, when it comes to getting along with others, confit is the most broad-minded of ingredients.

IT MAY NOT concern itself with duck or goose, but one of the Languedoc's best-known folk tales definitely centres on food. According to popular lore, when the people of Carcassonne were besieged by Charlemagne in the eighth century, the inventive Madame Carcase stuffed a pig with the citizens' meagre remaining supply of grain and insolently hurled it over the ramparts. Presented with such telling (and, I imagine, messy) evidence of abundance, Charlemagne abandoned the siege. Triumphant chimes rang out to salute Madame Carcase and the town was named "Carcase sonne" — "Carcase rings the bell" — in her honour. Apocryphal? Absolutely. The name probably comes from the Carsac plateau just south of the city, where settlements have been dated back to 400 BC.

    With its numerous turrets and towers and three kilometres of stone ramparts silhouetted on the skyline, the city of Carcassonne looks like a film set; which of course it often has been. But while Madame Carcase and her pig are immortalized on postcards sold everywhere within the picturesque city walls, you don't hear much about Eugène Emmanuel Viollet-le-Duc,

Carcassonne

the man who deserves most of the credit (or blame, depending on who you talk to) for the wonder that is Carcassonne. For the truth is that a considerable part of the city is a nineteenth-century restoration. An architect and writer, Viollet-le-Duc is best known for his repair work, which included Chartres cathedral and Paris' soaring Sainte Chapelle. This was a man who liked to keep himself busy. Even as he supervised the rebuilding of Carcassonne in the mid-1800s, he was working on France's greatest medieval cathedral, Notre-Dame-de-Paris.

We had built up such fantasies in our minds that, almost inevitably, our first visit to the city that had ignited the whole adventure was a letdown. We had anticipated crowds, but not the plethora of shops selling kid-size plastic armour, flouncy dolls and other cheap souvenirs. I wanted to slingshot myself back to the thirteenth century when Carcassonne was in its fighting prime as sentinel, fortress and war machine. Roaming the massive sandstone walls, I tried to pull apart the curtains of time, stretch the fabric of the centuries to a gossamer thinness that would let me feel how lonely and terrifying it must have been to be on patrol, high on the fortifications at midnight with an unprotected drop into darkness at my side.

By the mid-1800s the city was in a ramshackle state close to ruin, its structures crumbling, its stones pillaged by inhabitants building their own homes, the roofs of its towers long gone, degenerated into sheds, barns and chicken houses. The government stepped in, putting Viollet-le-Duc in command. The original Carcassonne had grown over the centuries, naturally, as an oyster does, accreting layer after layer, but Viollet-le-Duc moved fast on the huge restoration project, hence its perfection. He also — and historians grumble hugely over this — used slate for the roofs, which was neither typical of the place nor the era.

The illusory city we had concocted for ourselves back in North America was, in its own way, just as unreal as Viollet-le-Duc's reconstruction, and we felt little urge to return after our first visit in 1993. Subsequently, racing across the south on the *péage* (toll highway), we would sometimes see the giant coronet of Carcassonne's walls in the distance or the rearview mirror, but it was not until some years later that the Camelot that had first seduced us into visiting the Languedoc became actuality. It was far enough into autumn for tourist numbers to have dwindled and late enough in the afternoon for the sun to shoot rays horizontally on to the old city, gilding its cone-capped towers, dusting its walls with bronze and transforming it into a place of utter enchantment. This time, crossing the fourteenth-century bridge that spans the river, we could picture armoured knights, tournaments and gold-embroidered banners.

"So what do you think?" I said to Peter. "Was restoration on that massive a scale a good move or not?"

We paused, both to take photographs and to consider.

"I'm glad it was done when I see it from this bridge," said Peter, "but not so much when we're close up. It's too perfect."

Beyond the walled city flows the river Aude, and on the far side of the lower town is the Midi Canal, the man-made ribbon of water that completes the link between Atlantic and Mediterranean. To the north are endless vineyards. France's largest grape-producing region, the Languedoc produces an astonishing variety of wines, from headily sweet muscat to sparkling Blanquette de Limoux, not to mention hundreds of lusty reds and piquant whites made from grapes grown nowhere else. Yet it wasn't that long ago that the Languedoc name made oenophiles sniff — and not with appreciation. A grape-growing area since Roman times, the huge, almost unbroken vineyard spread out across the south had become notorious for churning out vast amounts of suspect plonk. By the mid-1950s, the French were beginning to drink less but better wine, and things slowly turned around. Encouraged by the government, growers planted new grape varietals, investors realized that the area was ripe for discovery, and wine-lovers discovered drinkable, and sometimes exceptional, labels at prices they could afford. These days, the area is touted as the vineyard of the future.

It's also the world's most colossal vineyard, stretching from the Banyuls *appellation* close to the Spanish border to the tiny region just west of the Rhône where the Clairette grape — once the leading white grape of the region — is still grown. Spreading along the *garrigue*, thick with mauve-grey hummocks of thyme and shoots of wild garlic, the Minervois *appellation* stands on the first hills of the Massif Central, the great hump of land that dominates central France. We had tasted some of these labels and read about others, but we were curious to hear the full story from someone whose life was wine.

A short drive from Carcassonne brought us to the gates of
the Château Villerambert-Julien estate to meet Michel Julien,
whose wine Robert had introduced us to on our first trip. With
his youth, blue jeans and energy, Michel typifies the new generation of Languedoc winemakers. The 68-hectare vineyard has
been in the Julien family since 1850, but
"a vineyard has stood on this site
since 1253," Michel told us, "and
possibly longer." At one time the
site was called Villa Rambertus,
and a plough once brought
to light plates and cups from
the fourth-century Gallo-
Roman period. For Michel,
change had meant planting
new varieties and using new
techniques. He showed us the
separator where the grapes are
"welcomed" into the winery and
stripped of their green stalky wish-
bones, astringent with tannins.

He has increased the density of the
vines — and lightened their load. "If I ask
you to carry fifty kilos," he explained, "it is
difficult. If I ask you to carry two kilos, you will dance as you
do it. If I ask a vine to produce a half-litre instead of three, it
has more flavour." Part of the estate is built from the same marble
used for some of the columns and fountains in the Trianon at
Versailles and the Opéra in Paris, names he once used in the

labels he produces (Trianon later had to be abandoned for copyright reasons). After we had tasted both, Michel drove us to the highest point of the vineyard so we could see for ourselves the giant white-striped blocks of pink marble lying in their quarry.

Authentique is a word we hear often in the Languedoc. More than just authentic, it means real in a way that's true to the land and its traditions. "This is an authentic region for wine," said Michel. "Here, it's not the fashion to make wine, it's natural." He spread his arms wide: "From Spain to the Côte d'Azur, it's all wine. Our sugar," he pointed to the sky, "is the sun." He might also have added that his wine, as we have discovered on several occasions since, makes a handsome accompaniment to a platter of duck confit.

These days it shows up on trendy menus, but never forget that confit's origins are modest: it's a simple, age-old way of preserving meat. In France, ducks come with their own thick fat overcoat. Elsewhere, cooks have to improvise — at least for the first batch. Stockpiling fat from a number of ducks is one possibility. Freeze it until you have enough to render, then add the fat and trimmings to a quarter cup of water and cook over low heat until the fat melts. Strain into clean containers and refrigerate. You can also ask your butcher if he knows of a source or, expense be damned, look for canned duck or goose fat at a specialty food store. Easiest of all is to use lard.

Cook confit very, very slowly. The fat should simmer as gently as a two-month-old baby blowing bubbles.

DUCK CONFIT

4	duck legs	4
3 tbsp	coarse salt	45 mL
1	bay leaf	1
2	garlic cloves, finely chopped	2
1 tsp	black peppercorns	15 mL

Enough duck fat, or a mixture of duck fat and lard
to cover (about 4 1/2 cups / 1.125 L)

Toss the duck legs with the salt and seasonings, cover and refrigerate overnight. The next day, pat the legs with paper towels to remove excess moisture and brush off any remaining visible salt.

In a tall deep pot just large enough to hold the duck legs, heat the duck fat until it "shivers." Gently insert the duck legs so that they are completely covered. Cover the pot and reduce the heat so that the fat remains at a steady slow simmer. Start testing with a skewer after one hour, to see if the meat is cooked.

Let duck legs cool slightly in fat, then place them in a large, spotlessly clean bowl (I rinse it with boiling water just before using). Reheat fat to simmering point and pour through a strainer over the legs so that they are completely covered. Cover bowl with foil and store in fridge. You can eat confit within one week, but its flavour matures as it ages.

To serve, bring bowl to room temperature and remove duck legs, letting as much fat drip off as possible. Heat oven to 350° F (175° C), place the confit in a shallow dish and heat through for 30 minutes. If you like, pop the legs under the broiler for five minutes to crisp the skin.

Remove any fat from the pan as the duck heats and use it to pan-fry parboiled potatoes. Serve with an assertively dressed green salad.

You can reheat, strain and refrigerate the duck fat for your next batch.

Serves 4

CHAPTER 2

Cassoulet

CASTELNAUDARY
AND THE MIDI CANAL

Why does everyone in North America live life at such a pace? This question often comes up for discussion when we're in France, usually over a lengthy meal. Here, with just about everywhere closing for lunch for two hours, you can't shop or see your bank manager, so there's little point in rushing through a sandwich. And somehow, I can't picture many French business types eating salade de poulet sandwiches at their desks, except maybe in Paris. What we were learning more and more were the virtues of slowness, whether it was a way of getting around that let you really see the countryside or lingering over a dinner that took long pleasurable hours to prepare. The fast-growing Slow Food movement was still in its infancy, but delving into the food of the Languedoc was already turning us into advocates.

Methods of making confit may be contentious but those arguments pale beside the discussions concerning the dish in which it's a prime ingredient: cassoulet. The citizens of Carcassonne have one version and the Toulousains have another with mutton, but most food-lovers agree that the town of Castelnaudary is where it all started. So for a couple constantly thinking about their stomachs, it was preordained that we make a pilgrimage as quickly as possible to what most believe is the wellspring of the real, *le vrai*, cassoulet.

Sturdy, nourishing and abundantly belly-filling, cassoulet is a natural outgrowth of agricultural life in the Languedoc, where biting winters demanded a rib-sticking dish that could simmer untended all day at the back of the fire. As it is made in Castelnaudary and most other places these days, cassoulet has three main ingredients: confit of duck or goose, dried beans and Toulouse sausage. Breadcrumbs contribute a crisp topping and herbs add flavour, but these are frills: originally, this was a dish invented by necessity and what was around. It might be country fare with no pretensions, but this alliance of meat and beans is alleged to be the ancestor of many other dishes, among them Boston's edible claim to fame (in one of her books, Julia Child translates cassoulet as "French baked beans") and the Quebecois *fèves au lard*. Following this train of thought to its logical conclusion, it's not absurd to deduce that cowboys' campfire beans and the canned variety that is the mainstay of British "caffs" are also both, albeit feeble, descendants.

Tasting cassoulet on its home turf required careful preparation. Making our way along the broad, prosperous boulevard that led to the central square, we arrived in Castelnaudary intending to have a late and minimal breakfast to tide us over until the hour of the bean. The bar where we ordered coffee was out of croissants so the owner directed me to a nearby *boulangerie*; I brought back, its butter already leaving transparent patches on the paper bag, a *specialité de la région*, a pastry that combines the individually minor crimes of almond paste, chocolate, a sugar glaze and a shower of flaked almonds into something approaching mortal sin. Now what was needed was a brisk walk around town.

The day happened to be a saint's day, a cause for celebration, a reason for eating. Stallholders lined the street by the marketplace offering samples of cheeses, breads and charcuterie. We nibbled away, especially (in the interests of research for our approaching cassoulet feast) at the Toulouse sausage which, grilled, resembles a coiled brown snake. Still with time to kill before lunch, we wandered up to a church (which was locked), down to the tranquil, tree-lined Midi Canal, and into a *brocante*, the French term for a shop that leans more towards second-hand finds than antiques. Back in the main square, in a moment as pictorial as it was mouth-watering, we watched a chef in his whites load up the trunk of his white convertible with flats of glistening scarlet strawberries. By now the temperature had climbed, but the long-awaited cassoulet was out of the question for another reason. The combination of pastry, samples, sausage and a shared slab of *pissaladière* (an anchovy-and-onion-topped tart that was just too tempting to pass up) had left us unfit to tackle a dish that can only be relished on a stomach so hollow it echoes.

Over the following years we tasted cassoulet in restaurants and out of jars, but it wasn't until the late nineties that we once more set out to tackle this rambunctious dish on its native ground. This time we trained for the event: omelettes and a frugal salad the night before and only half the usual amount of baguette barely

PLAT DU Jour
Cassoulet maison
"Le Bramais"
Volailles "PAY CATHARE"
crudités diverses
Plats cuisines journaliers
charcuterie-Salaisons
Conserves
Plats cuisines Chauds

smeared with butter and jam for breakfast. By the time we approached Castelnaudary, we were ravenous. Billboards promoted different canned varieties on the road into town. Out of sight, I imagined hungrily, were cassoulet factories processing stupendous swirling vats of the stuff, vats as large as the huge oval lake at the centre of the town known as *le Grand Bassin* whose shape, in a nice example of nature imitating cuisine, resembles the *cassole*, the brown, slant-sided pottery dish that gives cassoulet its name. To digress even further, also brown and slant-sided are the hats worn by the members of the Grande Confrérie du Cassoulet de Castelnaudary, a group of gourmets who convene solely to eat, and talk about, cassoulet. It's probably not coincidental that their robes are the hue of a grilled sausage and the yellow trim is remarkably close to the colour of duck fat.

A *cassole* was on display in the Castelnaudary tourist office, whose staff was generous with information but tight-lipped about which restaurant or shop made the most savoury dish. What they did give us was a map on which they X-ed several likely spots, one just across the street.

Au Gourmet Chaurien has shelves full of foods you want to scoop up and run home with: preserves made of quinces, melons, apricots or green tomatoes; terrines; foie gras; and jams made of red wine perfumed with thyme or green peppercorns, intended to accompany grilled meats, and a white wine version flavoured with lemon or pears and meant to be spooned over ice cream or used to perfume fromage blanc. But its main focus, witness the neon sign outside, is cassoulet. Here you can purchase the sturdy dish in quantities enough for one greedy eater or sufficient for a table of ten, and just about every size in between. When I expressed curiosity in the *cassoles*, Odile Laroche, the owner, told us they were made locally and provided the name of the pottery to add to our ever-growing list of places to visit next time. Her recipe? Traditional, of course, she replied, with no further elaboration.

Exactly what makes a cassoulet "traditional" is a subject of popular debate as heated as how to prepare the confit that is a core ingredient. Should one include tomatoes? And is it true that you must bury the breadcrumb crust (if you use one) below the bubbling surface seven times during cooking? And should the beans be *coco* beans from the town of Pamiers or *lingots* from Mazères or Lavelanet? Like Madame Laroche, all that Raymond and Margarita Escourrou, who run a store on a side street a few minutes away, would reveal is that their recipe has been used in the family business since 1963.

"Everyone makes their cassoulet a little differently," said Raymond, who incorporates pure pork sausage and confits of goose and duck into his. "It's like bakers who use different flours." As we talked and he fed us *fritons*, the crispy morsels of meat and fat left behind in the confit pot that make a delectable snack with aperitifs, the doorbell's "ping" punctuated the conversation. Usually alone, sometimes with kids in tow, a steady procession of women arrived bearing empty *cassoles*, which they

swapped for full ones, still warm, to take home for lunch. The oven is a relative newcomer to the Languedoc; you can still find houses where the cooking is done over open flames. Until recently, Raymond told us, people would sprint to the *boulangerie* or their village's communal oven to crisp their cassoulet's surface before taking it to the table.

The rush of customers had slowed and Raymond and Marguerite were about to close the store. We were more than ready for our own lunch. A quick scan of menus earlier had indicated no shortage of cassoulets, but it was the sign promoting a version cooked in a wood-fired oven that drew us into the busy Le Gondolier. We squeezed between chairs, secured one of the last empty tables, settled in with a *pichet* of wine and ordered two cassoulets. In the meantime, starving, I said to the waiter, perhaps a *salade Landaise*? In hindsight, a foolish move. It was a meal in itself, a mound of crisp greens with a slab of foie gras on top and other meats all around. We were ravenous enough to finish it down to the last chunk of confited *gésier* (gizzard) and crescent of smoked duck breast.

Then came the cassoulet, a steaming sea of pinky-brown beans broken by archipelagos of brown sausage and islands of confit and announced with a stentorian blast of garlic. Gutsy in flavour and texture, the sausage meat was coarsely chunked and stuffed so tightly into its skin that it exploded when I cut into it. The image of a fat woman undoing her corsets hovered briefly in my consciousness. Every bite was an experience, every bean perme-ated with meaty juices and aromatic with herbs. I searched for musical analogies but could find nothing suitably French. This wasn't the delicate structures of Debussy or Satie; it was brass bands, Wagner, the entire Ring Cycle, all of Beethoven's Nine played at full volume, and it was slowly, inexorably, anchoring me to my chair. Only by undoing my jeans could I mop up the last trace of juice. "*Terminé?*" asked the waiter. Very definitely.

lunch in Castelnaudary

du pain

Rosé

cassoulet avec porc et cuisse de canard

empty plate

As we lumbered out of the restaurant like pachyderms, passing a table where four slim girls sat with one cassoulet and four forks, I recalled the tale of the noted restaurateur Prosper Montagné who, on taking his shoes to the cobblers for mending, found the store shuttered and locked. On the door was a note: "Closed on account of the cassoulet." A perfectly reasonable explanation.

The town of Castelnaudary is more than just the fount of cassoulet; its *Grand Bassin* is also the main port of that engineering tour de force, the Midi Canal, a vital link in the system of waterways that slices right across southern France. Up until the seventeenth century, trade routes were sharply divided. Toulouse in the west shipped its saffron and woad to the Atlantic via the Garonne river, while in the south, silk from Nîmes, wool from Montpellier and cloth from Carcassonne were all funnelled into the Mediterranean. Sailors could steer a marine route between the two seas but only via the treacherous Strait of Gibraltar, a narrow death trap where pirates lurked knowing that ships had little means of escape. Mariners and merchants had dreamed of an unbroken channel across France for centuries; the missing link lay between the Mediterranean and the city of Toulouse.

Building the waterway would be a massive endeavour and only one man, Pierre-Paul Riquet, had both the imagination and the wherewithal to translate the stupefyingly ambitious scheme into reality. The practicalities didn't seem to bother him, perhaps because he was neither an engineer nor an architect; he had made his money collecting taxes on salt. I like to think of him, already in his mid-fifties, adding up columns of figures with only half his attention on what he's doing, his mind distracted by the map on the wall where he has inked a line to indicate the projected route of his marine highway.

Fervour alone could never have achieved it, but enthusiasm and financing are a strong combination.

Work began in 1666 and the Midi Canal opened fifteen years later, a silken green thread that still forms an unbroken channel between Sète on the Mediterranean coast and Toulouse, where it joins the Garonne river, which winds its way towards Bordeaux and into the Atlantic. The 254-kilometre project united experts in hydrography, topography, geometry, public works and architecture. And environmentalists: more than forty-five thousand trees, mostly planes and poplars, were planted to provide an endless summer parasol. Riquet was indomitable. Abrupt shifts in elevation, existing waters — nothing daunted him. He carved a tunnel 173 metres long through the mountain of Ensérune; he spanned rivers with aqueducts; he built a stairway of locks. Of course, the project inhaled money and, six months before it opened, Riquet died bankrupt.

What a legacy he left. The Midi Canal only closed to trade in 1988 and, more than three centuries after it was finished, it is still remarkably elegant, its long oval locks linked by stretches of jade green tunnels under their leafy umbrella. It seems impossible that the entire project was already a hundred years old by the time regal heads rolled in the French Revolution. We were struck by the canal's antiquity when we saw the diagonal grooves in the stone of the locks, etched by the rubbing of countless ropes, first of hemp, today of space-age fibres.

One summer, we helped dig them a fraction deeper. Back in France again, this time with eleven-year-old Kate, we had rented a small cottage less than an hour's drive from Castelnaudary, our embarkation point for a short voyage along the Midi Canal. Everyone had told us that handling a boat on the canal was so easy a child could do it. Well, not quite. The barge's maximum cruising speed, easily outpaced by joggers on the towpath, did mean that cruising along the canal involved little more than pointing the bow in the right direction, but negotiating the locks was more problematic.

When we picked up our vessel in Castelnaudary, athletic and experienced staff had shown us the ropes, literally, while helping us to navigate the first four locks, so by the final demonstration we believed we had the routine down pat. But we were only a few locks along the canal when Kate and I got the ropes tangled. Peter jumped off to help us; behind him the barge slowly dropped out of reach. We looked down on it, ten metres below, and realized that all we could do was lead it downriver by its ropes, like an enormous, clumsy puppy, to a point where we could board it again.

Steering a barge along the Midi Canal is similar to flying a plane. Separating the periods of deep, sleepy calm as you motor along at walking speed are the moments of frantic activity when you enter a lock. Here it is accepted etiquette to help the keeper turn the large handles that open the sluice and the gates of the lock. Lock-keepers put in intermittent workdays, to say the least, and the gardens of their cottages were brilliant with flowers. Invariably they shared their home with a dog: large, barking and chained, or small and *mignon* enough that the lock-keeper could hold Fifi or ZouZou in his arms while he opened the gates.

It was not all strenuous work. We took turns hopping off and idling along the towpath on foot or on the bikes we had brought along. Occasionally the canal came within sight of a distant road; the cars scuttling across the green fields looking like bugs on a billiards table, their evident hurry strangely incongruous. The non-marine world seemed a parallel universe, its checkerboard fields and blonde houses glimpsed through the trees like the flickering images of a turn-of-the-century zoetrope, the somnambulant pace of seven or eight kilometres an hour evoking straw hats, white linen, wind-up gramophones and wicker picnic baskets. Muzzy waterfalls of shadow from the trees over-head slid down the panelling in the forward cabin. Birds swooped across the bows and twittered in the background. The few boats we passed travelled at a similarly sleepy pace. You could sit on the roof reading, feet dangling through into the cabin. "A week of this," I wrote in my journal, "and I would be a blob."

The Midi Canal adheres to French time. Nothing happens between 12:30 and 1:30 p.m. and the locks are shut tight by 7:30 p.m., even in high summer, so that their keepers can sit down to dinner undisturbed. Our first night afloat, we leapt across a watery hedge of rushes and bright yellow irises and tied the ropes to two convenient trees at the side of the canal. For supper, prompted by a spicy chorizo I had bought at a market the previous day, I made a quasi-paella from the supplies we had brought onboard. Into the pan went sliced onions, plenty of garlic, two crimson peppers cut into rings, a fat tomato and a vast amount of rice — red, white and wild mixed together. We finished every last grain but were still hungry, so we downed the charcuterie and salad intended for tomorrow's lunch and only just kept our hands off the baguette meant for breakfast. Within minutes, we were dead to the world.

The next morning we anchored and strolled down a tree-lined road to a village to stock up on more pasta, more rice, and especially more bread. "Will two loaves be enough?" We recon-sidered and went back to the *boulangerie* for two more, devouring

one of them with cheese immediately in an impromptu picnic by the canal, watching the occasional fish "plop" through the surface of the greeny-brown water. Slaving away at lock gates and being out in the fresh air was giving us prodigious appetites. But still it wasn't enough: late in the day, aware of last night's gargantuan needs, we tied up yet again and walked along a narrow road into the oddly designed village of Bram.

From high above, Languedoc communities either resemble trees — with one main street and small roads branching off it — or are typical *bastide* towns, with a grid of streets and a central market square. Bram was different, built in concentric circles like the ripples created when you toss a pebble into a canal. It appeared tranquil today but the books I had brought along revealed it to be the site of one of the cruellest incidents in the Albigensian Crusade. As a terrible example to the Cathars, the crusader Simon de Montfort hacked off the lips, noses and ears of every soldier in the garrison at Bram and blinded all but one, who was left with a single eye so that he could lead the mutilated band, shuffling, sightless and agonized, to the fortress of Cabaret, which still held out against the invading army. Even today the story brings shudders, but we could see no ghosts in the glow of late afternoon sunlight. We ambled back to the canal along a roadside striped with tree shadows, crunching our way through grass dry as straw, our footsteps releasing whiffs of wild garlic.

To be afloat on the Midi Canal is to be a water-borne wanderer, a nomad creating a temporary home at the end of each day. That evening, after gigantic bowls of pasta, Kate returned from a bike ride along the towpath just as we finished washing the dishes. "There's English people over there," she said, pointing to the other side of the bridge, "and they say if you bring your glasses, they've got lots of wine." Which is how we came to meet Alan, a retired English lawyer, and his wife Bridget, who were en route from Bordeaux to the Greek Islands, and two young brothers from Norfolk taking a year off to roam. Instant friendships and unexpected honesties were created by plenty of *vin rouge* and the knowledge that we really were ships passing in the night. If the mosquitoes had not driven us back to our bunks, we all might still have been there the next morning, laughing, talking and passing the plastic *bidon* of red wine around.

Morning light on the canal turns the grass alongside the towpath to celadon green and bathes the houses in the pale gold of corn silk. The water is so undisturbed that it feels like the world around us is standing on a sheet of silver. In these side-by-side watery universes, there are no problems beyond handling the locks or anchoring to go in search of food. Our original plan when we left the *Grand Bassin* had been to go as far as we could, maybe even within sight of Carcassonne, but lulled by the tranquility, we were progressing at the pace of a large aquatic escargot. So on the second day, the captain ordered the crew to make the nautical move known to landlubbers as a U-turn and we headed back the way we had come.

At noon on our last day we arrived at the first of the four locks that brought us back to our starting point, Castelnaudary's *Grand Bassin*. At the last one, the water whooshed down in a great foaming, noisy mass that reminded me of footage I had seen of *The Maid of the Mist*, the boat that takes tourists to the base of Niagara Falls. Later, it was comforting to learn that the locks on the Canal du Midi are considered "violent." I realized that I had discovered the ideal balance of food intake and energy output. Working the locks on a regular basis was the only activity I knew that would burn off the calories in a typical cassoulet.

As with duck confit, there are as many ways to make cassoulet as there are people who make it. While I've lightened the following version considerably, it's still a substantial dish that needs no accompaniment except for a green salad afterwards and something ethereal for dessert. Even so, don't expect sparkling after-dinner conversation. Cassoulet is a powerful soporific.

CASSOULET

1 lb	boneless pork shoulder or butt, cut into cubes	500 g
1 lb	fresh garlic sausage, cut into large pieces	500 g
2	large onions, chopped	2
4	medium tomatoes, chopped	4
4 cups	dried white beans, soaked overnight and simmered just until tender, cooking water reserved	1 L
1 tsp	thyme	15 mL
1	bay leaf	1
4	garlic cloves, finely chopped	4
4	confited duck legs, cut apart at the joint, with some of their fat scraped off and set aside	4
4 cups	chicken stock	1 L
1/2 cup	fresh breadcrumbs	125 mL

Heat a large frying pan over medium heat, brown the pork cubes and set aside. In the same pan, brown the sausages in the pork fat. Return the pork to the pan, add the onions and tomatoes, reduce heat and cook the mixture for a few minutes until vegetables soften.

In a separate bowl, mix the cooked beans with the thyme, bay leaf and garlic. Adjust seasoning.

Preheat oven to 300° F (150° C).

Place half the bean mixture in a large casserole dish. Top with the meat mixture and arrange the duck on top. Add the remaining beans. Top up with chicken stock (and bean cooking water if needed) so the beans are almost covered. Bake for 1 hour.

Sprinkle with breadcrumbs and dot with reserved confit fat. Bake for 2 hours more until crumbs are browned and cassoulet is bubbling.

Serves 8

CHAPTER 3

Fine Fish and Peppers

BÉZIERS AND NARBONNE

Our few days on the Midi Canal had whetted our appetite for more. It wasn't just the languorous pace or the scenery, it was being able to cook for ourselves en route. During Vancouver's dismal winters, I would lay the map of France out on my desk and plan future voyages, timed strategically to take in as many markets as possible. The longer cruise still remains a fantasy, but "market research" is an ongoing project that has drawn us back again and again to the best "halles" in the region.

One day, we promise ourselves, we will journey along the entire length of the Midi Canal, west to east, Toulouse to the Mediterranean. But not the other way round, because the only stage of the waterway that intimidates us, and is thus best tackled late in the voyage, is Pierre-Paul Riquet's masterwork, the staircase of locks just outside Béziers. While honour dictated that his canal should wind a fond arm around his hilltop hometown, common sense suggested that rather than climb into the town itself, his waterway should skirt the base. Even so, Riquet was forced to create a link between two levels of water a mere 300 metres apart with an altitude difference of 21.5 metres, about the height of a six-storey building. His solution was seven locks, one right after another.

It was June and, European business trip over, I had managed to grab a couple of weeks for solo meandering in the Languedoc, riding trains from town to town to places I wanted to get to know better. One crystalline morning, the dream of boating along the entire Midi Canal at the back of my mind, I resolved to walk into the countryside just outside Béziers to see how daunting the locks of Fonséranes really were. Following the succession of small, steep streets that wind down from the town centre to the river Orb, I eventually joined a towpath alongside the canal. Four boats, gleaming white, waited in line to climb the first rung of Riquet's ladder. The shorts-clad lock-keeper closed the gates and, as the water rose, the boats bobbed like rubber ducks in a bath. One down, six steps to go. Up close and in reality, it didn't appear that intimidating.

I watched the methodical opening and closing until it was time for lunch, when I knew that all lock-related activity would grind to a halt, then purchased a pâté-stuffed baguette and

nabbed a table outside the small sandwich shop beside the canal. All of Béziers lay before me, the steep-sided hill town dominated by a massive cathedral, its tall square towers and bastion-like walls a landmark for miles around. No wonder Riquet ignored the challenges and picked a route for his canal that allowed the barge masters of long ago to admire the place of his birth.

Repaying the favour, Béziers trumpets its pride in its native son. The town's main street, a spacious pedestrian boulevard shaded by double rows of plane trees, bears his name, and midway along it stands a statue of the man himself. In his tall boots and cape he's a swashbuckling musketeer, though the insouciance is rather betrayed by his countenance. Brow furrowed and eyes cast down, his expression goes beyond desolation; his is the face of a man whose dream has been ground down by reality. Riquet's likeness is the only sombre element on this amply-proportioned walkway, a popular place to sit, stroll in the dappled light or eat in one of the tented cafés whose menus are a cook's tour of everyday food in this part of France. Couscous, *moules frites* (mussels and French fries), pizza — you find them all here, including a paella chain that makes one of its specialties not with rice, but with tiny lengths of pasta.

I'd eat in one or other of these cafés most evenings, happily solo, finding contemplation as pleasant as conversation. Often the fare got me thinking about the way that flavours and foods defy national boundaries and wander at will. Cross-currents of spices, waves of ingredients, had all flowed into the everyday cuisine here. Moroccan and Algerian immigrants from France's colonies to the south had popularized couscous. The French — and I wouldn't dare take sides on this — claim that pizza is not from Italy, but is instead descended from the anchovy-and-olive-laden *pissaladière* found further east along the southern

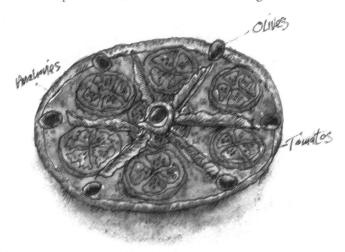

French coast; they think of it as profoundly French, *authentique*. A flyer I'd picked up somewhere listed a rustic version of pizza topped with lardons and *jambon de pays* and another, dubbed the *terroir* — a marvellous French word that encompasses soil, sun and rain and how they all affect what grows there — featured duck breast and *gésiers confits*. And then there was paella, not as out of place as it seemed. Even if I stayed in the slow lane (not that I had a car), I could join the *péage* at Béziers and be in Spain in less than two hours. Spanish, and especially Catalan, flavours seep far into France.

Over dessert, I considered my bowl of sorbet and wondered how the French produce such intensely flavoured but not overly sweet ones. Even the sorbets sold in supermarkets taste purely and simply of the essence of blackcurrants or pears.

"*L'addition, s'il vous plaît,*" and I knew that my bill would contain no surprises. I had chosen *le menu*, three courses for a set price, any taxes and the tip almost always included. I wondered why the concept of *le menu* has only crossed the Atlantic or the English Channel into higher-end restaurants. The French almost invariably order *le menu* or *table d'hôte* — the host's table — not just because it's the best value (three courses can cost as little as one ordered à la carte) but because this is where the freshest ingredients and ideas are to be found.

Typical of a *menu*, and of the region, is a meal I remembered enjoying with Peter in a side-street restaurant in Béziers during a previous stay. While I spooned up consommé with vermicelli, he downed a half dozen oysters. Hors d'oeuvres came next, *assortis*, which meant artfully cut radishes, a chunk of coarse-grained pâté, halved and mayonnaise-coated eggs and slices of both tomatoes and vinaigrette-dressed onion. The main course was *rognons en brochette*: "pork kidneys," elaborated our red-haired flirt of a waitress. Still rosy at their centres, they came with a sizzling heap of *frites*. We finished with poached pears with chocolate sauce and crème caramel. Good plain food, all of it, nothing pretentious but with each ingredient carefully chosen and thoughtfully cooked.

Often when we're in Béziers together we go to the bistro at
the corner of Place Jean Jaurès (whose central fountain is shaped
like a fluted, slope-sided dessert), a few steps from our favourite
hotel, the Hôtel d'Angleterre. (Modest prices and comfortable
beds apart, we usually stay here for two other reasons: the pleasant
owner who, one sweltering day, made me the gift of two Spanish
fans; and the vast stack of reading material by the reception desk
that, excavation reveals, almost always contains English magazines
of considerable vintage.) With its mural of lavender fields, the
bistro is a congenial place to while away the early evening over a
pression (draft beer). Outside, a palm tree partly hides a small stall
selling shellfish.

"*Coquillages*," I said out loud to Peter on one visit, reading the sign and pronouncing each syllable with pleasure. "It sounds so appropriate to the thing it describes, armoured on the outside, soft when you get into it." We agreed that "*poisson*," the French word for fish, had a suitably fleshy feel, unprotected by hard consonants. We were deep into gastro-etymological reveries concerning the sensual pleasures of saying *crème fraîche* and *foie gras* — preferably to a waiter — when a cloud burst suddenly with

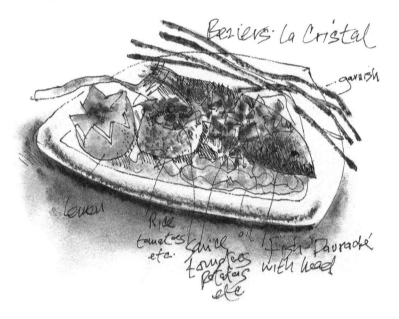

enormous force, as if a cauldron had tipped over high up in the clouds. Ladlefuls of water bounced off the pavement and its dark surface bubbled. Wielding a massive Coca-Cola umbrella, a waiter raced across the street to rescue a colleague stranded in the restaurant tent.

Besides being the city's chief dining strip, Allées Paul Riquet is also, at night, the place to promenade back and forth with your mate, your friends or your family, beneath the garlands of multicoloured lights strung overhead. In mood, it's as animated as the Ramblas in Barcelona. Balancing loaded trays at shoulder height, waiters manoeuvre through the Renaults and Citroëns that speed between the sidewalk restaurants and the canvas dining marquees along the central pedestrian section; lit up inside after dark, the tents look like a medieval encampment.

On Fridays the Allées are transformed into a flower market. By eight in the morning, trays of plants form a vividly patterned rug of pink, vermillion and creamy-yellow hibiscus, geraniums as dark as red wine, purple petunias and patches of impatiens in white, magenta, salmon and the crimson of a cardinal's robe. On the tables blaze pots of orange and yellow calendulas, their massed petals as frilly as can-can dancers' petticoats. Planks supported on upended metal buckets hold buckets of fuchsias, tall stiff gladioli and Van Gogh bunches of sunflowers. Hanging baskets are hooked on a stout cord slung between a handy tree and a lamppost. One stallholder presides over a miniature landscape of herbs, the meadows of chives, parsley, Genovese basil and tarragon broken only by tall spires of grey-green rosemary. But these are the only edibles on display: for produce you go to the Friday market under the trees at Place David d'Angers. Like any *marché* in France, this one was easy to find. All I did was stalk people carrying empty baskets; when I met others whose baskets were full going the other way, I knew that I was heading in the right direction.

Even if I shut my eyes as I walk around this, or any other, French market, I am still aware what stalls are nearby from the salty marine aromas of small red *rougets* and steel-coloured mackerel and the vinegary, nose-tickling gusts from the display of olives. Farther on were the hunger-inducing smell of rotisserie chicken and the harem perfume of opulent Charentais melons. A pungent whiff rose from a stack of onions, large, flattish and still attached to their green stems: SWEET ONIONS FROM LÉZIGNAN-CORBIÈRES said the sign. From a stall at the corner whispered the honeyed scent of *tilleul* (linden flowers), dried to pale fragility and enclosed in crumpled brown paper bags — "to help you sleep," said the sweet-faced woman with long grey hair who was minding the stall.

The market is the emotional heart and stomach of a French town. You buy what the stallholders sell; a shopping list is redundant. I watched a woman engage in discussion over cuts of beef, and another carefully select a punnet from an entire stall laden with strawberries, so ripe that their fragrance and scarlet gleam were quite irresistible. These were strawberries that you knew would be red to the core and would drip with juice. Why is it, I thought, that we even bother with out-of-season fruits with their pallid interiors and lack of flavour? Why not celebrate strawberries when they're in their prime, feast on them, gorge on them, bathe in them, and then dream of them until their moment in the annual cycle rolls around again?

I thought about markets too and how long ago, all towns and villages of any size were built around two structures: the church and the market square. How was it that the supermarket had taken over, anonymous, generic, a place where you would never stop to chat with stallholders, a temple to commerce and convenience that had nothing to do with taste and pleasure, lacking the faintest aroma of food except for piped-in bakery smells from the half-baked loaves trucked to the back of the store each morning? And I thought about the widespread success of farmers' markets in North America and the irony that the New World, having rejected many of its values, was now embracing the way of the Old.

Market and church. Body and spirit. Béziers has, of course, both. Religiously speaking, it also has a giant stain on its history. In 1209, the year that Pope Innocent III launched his attack on the Cathars, crusaders captured Béziers and slaughtered the men, women and children who had sought sanctuary in its churches. Legend says that as many as 20,000 were put to the sword by soldiers instructed to "kill them all: God will know His own." The *rues* that spiral away from the cathedral are constricted and steep, steep enough to let you believe that, as the story goes, the gutters ran with blood flowing down the slopes to the river.

All that gore seemed unimaginable one summer Sunday morning. Hours before, we had been kept awake by singing from the ebullient Saturday night crowd. Now Peter and I were searching for a *boulangerie* or café that was open. Usually hard at work by 7 a.m., even the small trucks that sprayed the streets (and sometimes our ankles), leaving both sidewalks and feet fresh and cool in their wake, were absent. The air was chill under the trees; the chairs from the outdoor restaurants were stacked. His last night's revelry now long over, a visibly hung-over man stared moodily at his beer in the café where we stopped for coffee. Only the occasional staccato clack-clack of high heels broke the silence as, dressed for church, the good women of Béziers headed towards the cathedral on the arms of their suit-clad husbands.

Curiously invisible from within the town, the cathedral of St. Nazaire is a mighty presence from up close. A fortress in appearance and position, its viewpoint encompasses the river Orb, the Midi Canal and, far in the distance, the orderly pinstripes of vineyards, randomly buttoned with villages. As we made our way into the square where it stands, a man cycled in at speed, a white surplice slung over his shoulder. In a single fluid movement he swerved towards the porch, braked, dismounted, hefted his bike on his shoulder and vanished into the throng at the cathedral door.

The bells began to peal and we merged with the crowd filtering in to the cathedral: the formally attired couples we had noticed earlier; teens in denim; a toddler clinging to a stuffed tiger. Elegant in beige linen and sporting pearl earrings like small full moons, a woman loped in with model-like grace, genuflected, tanned knee to the stone, then loudly embraced the couple in the pew in front of her. Midway through the service, two young girls dressed in fashionably skimpy outfits sidled in, conscious enough of protocol to shrug jackets over their bare shoulders but still young enough to erupt into helpless giggles that drew fingers to pursed lips from their neighbours. This was the day for the baptisms of Brandon, Clémence and Jérémie, and a day for first communions too. Pursued by video-recording relatives and camera flashes, Mélodie, Jonathan, Julie and Julien all stood solemnly, dressed up and polished till they shone, relishing their turn in the religious limelight. The service was over within half an hour. We threaded our way through the family groups, knowing that they were probably off to a celebratory Sunday lunch.

Our turn for a long midday feast didn't come until two days later, when we said goodbye to Madame at the hotel, packed up the car and headed northeast towards the vineyards. Whichever direction you leave Béziers from, you cross wine country. It stands in the Coteaux du Languedoc region, an *appellation* that now draws attention from such overseas wine concerns as the Australian BRL Hardy company. We had met Nigel Sneyd, who worked for Hardy at the time, at Vancouver's annual international wine festival, where he was representing the company's Domaine de la Baume. We had tasted some of his wines, got into conversation and, when he heard about our forthcoming visit to France, he had asked us to lunch.

An enthusiastic cook, Nigel had risen early to raid Béziers' indoor market, and when we followed him into the kitchen, we saw all his plunder laid out on the kitchen counter.

"What are these?" I pointed to what looked like a bundle of old-fashioned razor cases — or the razor clams I was familiar with on the Pacific coast.

"They're called *couteaux* — knives," he said. "They're a type of shellfish, and you only get them around here at certain times of the year."

I wanted his kitchen with its terra cotta tiles, open wood oven and a window that looked out on rows of Cabernet and Merlot vines. On the shelves stood jars of curry leaves, candlenuts, dried galangal and garam masala. Sneyd likes to cook Indian food and like most Australians or Brits who have grown up surrounded by multicultural cuisine, he had quickly tracked down nearby sources. Draining in the sink were what appeared to be small lengths of seaweed, vividly green and as glossy as bottle glass. "It's *salicorne*," he explained, a salty vegetable, some-times called glasswort, that grows in the Camargue.

Into a big frying pan went olive oil, followed by some of the new season's garlic, tarragon from a window box that also held mint, thyme, chives and sage, and a slosh of Sauvignon Blanc. Then in went the *couteaux*. "These little fellows are interesting," said Nigel. "This is a total experiment." Meaty, tender and sweet, they were outstanding.

In its first years, the new methods of winemaking that Nigel undertook were viewed with suspicion, he told us as we finished the last of the *couteaux*. "Now," he said, "I've heard 'we work by the Hardy method,'" which means that the grapes destined for white wine, which are brought in from as far away as Sète and Perpignan, are picked as late in the day as 10 p.m., or as early as two in the morning, a technique borrowed from north-ern France. "We were the first to do night-picking, in 1991." Ingredients, technique, timing. "It's like being a chef," he added as he turned his attention to the tuna steaks; "the philosophy is the same."

Pan-seared in olive oil, the fish went into the oven, topped with sliced fresh limes, a thin layer of tomato sauce, onions, red pepper, lemon thyme and tomatoes, the last from the garden of resident winemaker Jérôme Girard, who also provided Nigel with courgettes, aubergines, salad greens, radishes and pumpkin, depending on the season. Lunch wound up with Roquefort from a small local producer and a bowl of juicy black cherries. Go to the market, buy what looks good and treat it simply. Whether you're winemaker, chef or visitor, it's a recipe that never fails whatever Languedocien town or village you're in.

A few years later I found myself in the ancient city of Narbonne, on the flower-lined banks of the Canal de la Robine west of Béziers. The prome-nade along the waterway is notably pleasant, past cafés and patisseries and tall, pale-stuccoed houses, their windows outlined in primrose yellow or shuttered in maroon. You can even, if you must, down a McEspresso. But why would you, when you can go to the market instead?

On this occasion I was travelling solo, which meant without a car; I have yet to drum up the nerve to drive in France. I had come here for the day from Béziers, walking along the long boulevard that led from the station and turning into the street that ran beside the canal. I'm of two minds as to which indoor market is better, the one in Béziers or the one in Narbonne, which provides sensual harassment from the moment you go inside and see dark green peppers with burnt orange stripes, almost as long as your forearm, or perfectly marbled cuts of beef wrapped in thin opaque overcoats of fat.

Warm with pleasure, I wandered from stall to stall, not knowing what to watch or taste first. The day was still young and I had hours to spare before I had to catch the train back to Béziers. Wielding a blowtorch, a young man flamed chickens to burn off errant feathers. A farmer's wife, promoting an approaching rural event, handed out samples of bread spread with fresh cheese and smoky honey. Wearing shorts, striped shirt and tweed hat, a man in horn-rimmed glasses, hands behind his back, looked on approvingly as a butcher sawed off the hock from a hanging carcass. And, in the large open area at the centre of the market, a festival of the locally caught eels was underway.

Three big gas rings flamed like the rings of Jupiter. Over them, tossing each pan in turn, a rotund bearded chef, his sweat-drenched hair like licorice strings, sautéed thumb-length pieces of eel in pans so huge he needed to use both hands, protecting them from the heat with a red-and-white checked cloth. Using his thumb to block the neck of the bottle and control the flow, he drizzled pastis over each pan and set light to the alcohol. Flames jumped a metre high, then died just as abruptly, and he sprinkled the now-finished dish with a handful of chopped parsley from a yellow plastic bucket. Beside the stall, shoppers lined up to buy *barquettes* (little tubs) of eel and potatoes to take home. Damn, I wanted a small stone cottage, or rather its kitchen, to take them home to.

Near the eel-cooking area, a large display explained the life cycle of the *anguille d'Europe*: the European eel. Females grow up to a metre and a half long, I learned, can weigh two kilograms and live for twenty years. Males are frail in comparison, growing only one-fifth as long, weighing a tenth as much and being lucky if they live to see their ninth birthday. But enough biology. The third display panel, devoted to *la gastronomie*, talked of a *civet d'anguilles* made with onion, carrots, celery, wine and bouquet garni; *la bourride*, a stew of eel and potatoes eaten with garlicky bread; and the *anguilles persillées* that I had watched being prepared.

Over at the fish stall I checked out the whole eels, grey-white underneath and the same deep ferny green on top as the walls of the locks on the Midi Canal. Beside them lay tuna, its flesh the deep red of Merlot, pale pink-striated rays of skate and a motley collection of fish too small to cook on their own gathered under the *soupe de poissons* category. "What do you do with *violets*?" I asked the stall-holder. They looked like chunks of dark rock, rugged as oysters, dark and barna-cled. She demonstrated. Squeeze them and swallow the juice that squirts out, then break them open and eat what's inside. Good for the eyes, she said. I tried one later. They have a powerful iodine-y flavour.

Like any self-respecting French town, Narbonne boasts its own signature pastry: the Narbonnaise, a cake made with *fruits confits* and *crème pâtissière* and snowy with sugar. One stall sold those, large and small, and another displayed cakes sliced open to show green speckles of olives and pink chunks of ham. Yet another stallholder had whole hams for sale, the hoof still attached as in Spain, a reminder of how close this part of France is to the border. "Try it," he said, offering me a sliver on the blade of his knife. The ham had a complex taste and a nuttiness that lingered on my tongue. Elsewhere was evidence that Asian cuisine is — very, very slowly — finding a place on the French dining table. Here to take home — "assuming you're lucky enough to have a home in France," I thought enviously — were vegetable rolls, chicken with ginger and duck with pineapple. You could buy fresh ravioli, too, filled with goat cheese or Roquefort, and the cheese stall sold varieties I'd never seen before: La Brique des Etangs, a cow's milk cheese shaped like a thick chocolate bar; Bouton d'Oc, a tall pyramid with a length of matchstick stuck in its peak that gave it a shape like a small pear; and *boutons de culotte*, whose name, literally "knicker buttons," was a clue to their size. "A cheese for dolls?" I joked. The store owner laughed, then grew solemn. "But they are delicious," she said.

And they were.

Fresh eels are difficult to find but the dish I saw made in the market at Narbonne works equally well with cod, snapper or other firm white fish.

FISH NARBONNE-STYLE

2 tbsp	olive oil	30 mL
1 tbsp	butter	15 mL
4	thick cod fillets, about 6 oz (200 g) each	4
2 tbsp	parsley, finely chopped	30 mL
2	garlic cloves, finely chopped	2
	Salt and pepper	
2 tbsp	Pernod or other anise-flavoured liqueur	30 mL

Over medium-high, heat olive oil and butter in large frying pan. Add fillets and cook five minutes on each side, or till just done.

Sprinkle with garlic and parsley. Warm Pernod in a small saucepan, spoon over fish, and ignite. Once flames have died down, serve with sautéed new potatoes.

Serves 4

Glossy scarlet peppers are an irresistible buy, and cooked with onions and garlic, they make a versatile dish that goes well with most meats and fish, and shines as a starter. Equally delicious warm, cold or at room temperature.

MARKET PEPPERS

1/2 cup	good olive oil	125 mL
6	red bell peppers, seeded, and cut into wide lengthwise strips	6
2	large onions, halved and cut into crescents	2
12	cloves (or more) garlic, peeled	12

Heat oil in a large frypan and add peppers, onion and garlic. Sauté gently until vegetables are tender-crisp. Tip contents of pan, including juices, into bowl. If not serving immediately, cover and refrigerate.

Serves 6 as a side dish

CHAPTER 4

Martinis and Mussels

MARSEILLAN AND SÈTE

I start adding to "the France File" the moment I get back from each trip. In it go snippets of information: addresses, business cards, wine labels, clues to help us delve deeper into the Languedoc's food and wine on our next visit. This was the year that martinis had become the de rigueur cocktail. Fruit-based spin-offs showed up. As a judge at a martini contest, I even tasted a version made with shavings of fresh truffles. Enough, I thought, and started thinking about the classic original version, which led to a little research. Soon I was running my finger over our increasingly frayed map of the Languedoc. "Look," I said to Peter, "it's only a three-hour drive from that house we'll be renting. And then there's that winery in the abbey ..."

Narbonne is the coastal crossroads of the Languedoc, the *gare* where you change trains and where the wide grey bands of major highways strap together, their names befitting their destinations. The Catalan snakes south through the mountains to Spain, while the western arm of The Highway of the Two Seas follows much the same route as Riquet's great canal to Toulouse before turning towards Bordeaux and the Atlantic Ocean. If we stayed with its eastern arm we would eventually meet the Rhône, but one late September day we branched off on a side road soon after the final exit sign for Béziers. Our destination was Marseillan. Drowsing in the afternoon sun, this serene little port lies at the southern end of the Etang de Thau, one of the huge lagoons that stretch along the coast between here and the Camargue, the Rhône's massive and marshy delta, like a necklace of gigantic elongated pearls.

Marseillan is a fishing community, and what action there is there centres on the small rectangular harbour near the spot where the Midi Canal flows into the Etang. Many of the town's 4,000 inhabitants are involved in harvesting the oysters and mussels raised in the Etang de Thau; only a handful work at the unassuming factory at the end of the harbour. But their impact is immeasurable, for the elixir they produce is the root of the Western world's best known cocktail. Ta-da; pause for flourish of trumpets. For Marseillan is where Noilly Prat vermouth is made, the vermouth used in the first martini created in the early 1900s by bartender Martini di Arma di Taggi in New York City. We felt we should drop to our knees; or better still, hoist ourselves onto bar stools.

A lifelong fan of the martini, I had always been puzzled by Ogden Nash's classic poem lauding "a yellow, a mellow martini."

Wasn't a classic martini supposed to be flawlessly clear? The thought nagged at me. I knew that the accepted ratio of vermouth to gin used to be considerably higher than today's mere allusion, but surely the vermouth had to be the colour of gold if it was to noticeably tint the gin. However, if I thought we could track down the answer to my question right now, I was mistaken. It was late in the day and the Noilly Prat facilities were tightly capped.

Oh well, we had planned an overnight stay anyway. Right at the harbour's edge stood the Château du Port, looking like an enormous doll's house, its orderly windows trimmed with wrought iron balconies and a top row of dormer windows protruding from what must once have been the servants' quarters. Inside was fresh and sunny, with walls painted a warm yellow and abundant white rococo trim like the icing on a wedding cake. High above, an oval-domed skylight framed with painted flowers spilled light down a splendid curving marble staircase. The steps that led to the top floor were of terra cotta tiles and the beams, ceiling and walls in the attic room — all that our budget would stretch to — were painted gleaming white. There was even a view of the water, if we craned our necks out the window past Monet-flowered curtains.

An antique engraving on the cover of the hotel's brochure depicts a quayside lined with rows of barrels and, in the far distance, the masts and sails of seagoing clippers. By the time the hotel was constructed, towards the end of the nineteenth century, Marseillan's vermouth industry was already well underway. The story is a romantic one. An *aromatiste* for a perfume company, a certain Monsieur Joseph Noilly, was not the first person to create a drink of herbs and wine (the ancient Romans and

Greeks had beaten him to it), but in 1813 he did have the foresight to found a company in Lyon. Serendipity played a role
when he hired a Monsieur Claudius Prat as his coach driver.
Prat fell in love with Noilly's daughter, married her, and, in
1843, was adopted into the company by his father-in-law, who
had meanwhile been busy clearing the Marseillan area of mosquitoes, building a factory and constructing a port. With the
Midi Canal and the Mediterranean Sea on the doorstep, business
blossomed, and Noilly Prat was soon in the export business.
A showcase in the factory, which we visited the next day, shows
a certificate from Washington, DC, dated 1883, registering the
trademark for Vermouth, a trademark that would be in effect
for thirty years.

The grapes whose juices merge in Noilly Prat vermouth
are two obscure varietals: the lively Picpoul de Pinet and the
heavier, nuttier Clairette du Languedoc. Grown within fifty kilometres of Marseillan, both are matured separately and then —

still kept apart — aged indoors for twelve months in barrels, three metres across, of Canadian oak that contains white, not red, sap and therefore doesn't colour the wine. The wine is then decanted to smaller barrels and left for a year — "four seasons is more important than twelve months," the vermouth-makers tell you — outside in the blazing sun, where temperatures can climb to forty-two degrees Celsius. About eight percent, "the angel's share," evaporates.

The reason behind the "yellow martini" was becoming apparent. The vermouth shipped to North America these days is only a year old and almost colourless, the wines that have aged and yellowed in the sun making up a mere ten percent of its content; the other ninety percent has been kept indoors. All the wines that go into the more golden European version have spent their time basking outdoors, and the vermouth continues to age in the bottle, getting darker and darker until it is more like Madeira in taste. North Americans like their vermouth to be pale; Europeans don't. It's as simple as that. So, technically speaking, unless you can get your hands on European vermouth, you can't drink a martini as it was originally invented.

Making vermouth is not overly labour intensive. The bottling is done elsewhere: only twenty people work in the factory in Marseillan, one of them at the computer that oversees the all-important blending that takes wine down the road to becoming vermouth. I leaned over the operator's shoulder and looked at the abbreviations on the screen. "Alc" was self-explanatory: alcohol. "Cit," he told me, was short for *citron* and "Fra" was code for *framboise*. They distill the lemon and raspberry *eaux-de-vie* on the spot, adding them to the aged wine and *mistelle* (natural wine sugar) to create the base for vermouth.

What gives vermouth its distinctive flavour, of course, are the herbs. The dry white version contains nineteen plants; the sweeter red vermouth is a mélange of twenty-three. Not far from the inhuman efficiency of a computer was a room that flashed us back to the nineteenth century and that smelled, as did much of the factory, like the inside of a Christmas pudding. Stacked on the floor were sacks of nutmeg, quinine bark and dried Spanish orange peel. There was oregano, cinnamon, bay leaves, dried pink rose buds from Holland, cloves from Madagascar, yellow chamomile flowers redolent of honey and pale coriander seeds from Morocco, everything weighed by hand on a small old-fashioned scale and combined according to the original 1813 recipe. Two sackfuls of the aromatic mixture are added to each barrel. Then, for two minutes each day for six weeks, a worker opens the lid and moves the herbs and flowers around with a small scythe-like tool. I could not imagine a less taxing or more pleasant job to be found anywhere.

The European host pours his vermouth more as an aperitif than as a mix, but sixty percent of it is used not for drinking but for cooking. I too had caught the bug. Having abandoned the hotel life as too frustrating for passionate cooks, we were now renting cottages and I was on a bender, culinarily speaking. My daube and beef bourgignon contained lashings of red wine, a glug of white added flavour to the fish stock and extravagant splashes of muscat livened up a dish of baked apples. This alcoholic profligacy in the kitchen was one of the aspects of France I most missed when I was back in Canada where, a small nod to the government for this, wine prices are among the highest in the world. On North American soil, I have become a convert to vermouth as an all-purpose vinous seasoning, and I'm not alone.

According to the Noilly Prat company's promotional literature, chefs from temples of epicurianism as lofty as Maxim's and Lucas-Carton in Paris use it in their dishes.

I never did find out if our lunch at the endearing La Table d'Emilie was tinged with vermouth — or who Emilie was, for that matter. But she certainly had beguiling taste. Installed in an ancient building with a vaulted stone ceiling, her restaurant was intimate in size and mood, with a small plant-filled conservatory off the main room and nimble waitresses dashing to and fro. While we mulled over the lunch menu, there was pixie food to divert us: tapenade squiggles on pastry squares the size of a thumbnail. Then, dish by dish, our order arrived. First up was a serene oval of crab mousse on a lake of tomato essence touched with cayenne. Next were svelte foie gras slices, pale with a few jewels of blood and served on crisp sautéed potatoes, followed by squid, tender and sweet in a sauce of butter and new garlic. Then came monkfish with carrots, each slice apparently cut with pinking shears, and a tangle of julienned courgettes. I dithered over the cheese tray's thirty or so varieties before choosing a selection of *chèvres*, young and sprightly, old and raunchy, to go with the walnut bread. All this before dauntingly rich ice cream studded with pistachios on a sea of red berry coulis, a single red currant here, plum slices there. Late in the afternoon, while the rest of the world was travelling at normal speed, we ambled back along the quay in what felt like slow motion, the placing of each foot on the ground a carefully considered act.

La Table d'Emilie remains on our list of places to eat at whenever we're in the area. At one dinner, the *amuse-gueule* (tastebud teasers) included the tiniest spinach quiches I've ever seen and single stuffed mussels resting on a reduction of seafood stock swirled with cream that looked like liquid marble. Sampling continually from one another's plates, we tasted oysters on a bed of seaweed and a buttery carpaccio of salmon, its fanned slices decorated with julienned cucumber and a dollop of crème fraîche peppered with poppy seeds, completed by a harlequin decoration of precisely cut diamonds of red and yellow pepper around the rim of the plate. The mysterious "Montgolfier" on the menu turned out to be an individual tureen topped with an air-puffed balloon of pastry concealing shrimp in a curry cream sauce. The dessert — nougat ice cream slowly melting into its puddle of raspberry coulis garnished with strawberry slices, mint leaves, black grapes and cherries — was so beautiful that Peter sketched it on the spot.

While La Table d'Emilie could stand its ground in Paris or any other food-centric city, not all dining in Marseillan attains such a level of urban panache. One summer Sunday evening we followed the sound of music to its source, a small procession of men in braid-trimmed red jackets, black pants and straw boaters and women in flowered skirts. A coach and horses clip-clopped along. We were invited to join them for songs and dances of Poland, *un grande spectacle,* free at the local theatre, and we would have gone except that under the plane trees in another square, four spitted lambs slowly revolved over fires of gnarled vines, part of the celebrations of a Fête du Cheval (horse festival). Elvis pumped out "Jailhouse Rock," kids wandered around clutching cans of cola and Orangina and, as the smoke rose, a man threw handfuls of salt over the meat, then, using a rag tied to a broom handle, swabbed on more marinade. Judging by what I could see on the oilcloth-covered table, garlic and tomato paste were its major components. We would have paid our sixty francs (this was before the euro) and joined the queue, except that we were expected at eight at Emilie's table.

Now that we have our own house in southern France, we of course have a wine cellar, a small corner in the reliably cool pantry; its contents, like Peter and I, don't wander far beyond regional boundaries. Why would they, when the staggering variety of terroirs means that Languedoc wines can take you from pre-dinner snacks through to dessert? (It's important to follow the rules in France: sweet muscat, for instance, is normally drunk as an aperitif, as I deduced from the waiter's puzzled look — "are you sure, Madame?" — when I ordered it one night as a post-dinner liqueur.) We often offer house guests flutes of sparkling Blanquette with a dash of *crème de cassis* — the low-rent version of kir royal — or a drink called *hypocras* that smells of spices and plums and is said to date back to medieval times.

Wine and history have been inextricably mingled in the Languedoc since the first century BC, when the Romans planted vines, and themselves, from the Rhône to the Pyrenees. Just seven kilometres from the sea and a mere half-hour from Marseillan stands the Abbaye de Valmagne, its great church, almost a cathedral in scale, dominating the skyline, an ecclesiastical ship in an ocean of greenery. A vineyard has stood on this spot "forever" according to the current owner, Diane de Gaudart

d'Allaines, whose family has lived at the abbey since 1840 and who told us that it dates back to 1139, when it was built by the Vicomte de Béziers. The first Romanesque church was reconstructed in Gothic style in 1257. The middle part of the abbey is late seventeenth century and was built as a *logis*, a spot for pilgrims to stay on their way to Compostela.

Madame spoke of the ancient abbey with the familiarity and affection of someone describing the home they grew up in. Outside the abbey church she pointed out the stone hollows for holy water and the grapes and vine leaves carved over the main door. "Poor people used to drink a lot of wine — four, five, six litres a day in the early nineteenth century," she explained as she pointed to the huge barrels inside, snugged along the sides of the church. These days, this lofty space large enough to accommodate a hundred and seventy singers, seventy musicians and an audience of nine hundred is often used for music festivals and concerts. The refectory with its stained-glass windows is the site of wine tastings, she told us, and the mantelpiece is Renaissance from a castle on the Rhône. The marble floor? "This is modern, this is the nineteenth century."

Her comment touched a chord in both of us. Here was part of the authenticity we were seeking. Living in a city barely a century old, where the few old buildings had long been torn down by developers, we missed the sense of history that was part of everyday life here. With every visit, we'd "lick the windows" of real estate agents' offices, gradually acquiring a vocabulary that enabled us to interpret the brief descriptions. *Ancien* meant, well, ancient, but in most cases, no one knew exactly how ancient. A *villa* was the code word for something built in modern times, the last thing we were looking for. But we did have to be realistic.

Tempting though it was to take on a huge but inexpensive ruin, we lacked the practical skills required to renovate it. Our manual know-how ceased at the keyboard and canvas.

What we did know by now was that this was where we wanted to settle, if only for part of the year. Why this area? Talking about it we realized that, in many ways, it would be like returning to our roots. I had grown up in a medieval town with a market square, a dominant cathedral and a grid of little streets overhung with half-timbered houses; though English, it was remarkably like many *bastide* communities in the Languedoc. Peter was born in Montreal, a predominantly French-speaking city whose history dates back to the 1600s. And then there were our ancestors: mine were farmers and butchers; Peter's had sailed over from France in the early seventeenth century, and genealogical research by his brother suggests they might have hailed from the Languedoc. That this area, with its profound passion for food, felt so much like home was hardly surprising. In a sense, it was in our genes.

The "if it's new, it must be better" ethos of North America was starting to pall, too. Here houses weren't bulldozed flat in a day and their materials carted off to the landfill. Stone homes might collapse eventually but stone could be used over and over again. As environmentalists, we liked that, as we liked the way that structures, from small cottage to large ecclesiastical properties, evolved over the centuries. Like fine wines, they grew more interesting as they aged.

Outside in the sunshine, we sauntered around the cloisters of the Abbaye de Valmagne, which are built on a Roman site and frame a moss-covered fountain that is part of the original abbey, where monks washed their hands before mass or meals. Madame regaled us with stories of riding around the cloisters on her bicycle as a little girl, as she opened a bottle, motioned us to sit by the fountain, and poured us a glass. It was full of fruit and character, smelling deliciously of red and black currants. The wines go with all sorts of red meats, she tells us, and are very good with cheese and chocolate. "We've got good soil and we've got the sun," she said, a woman proud of her region (echoing what Minervois winemaker Michel Julien had told us when we visited him near Carcassonne). "In Bordeaux it rains every day."

Not far from the Abbaye de Valmagne, a tiny *appellation* in the Coteaux de Languedoc region produces the ancient grape variety used to make Picpoul de Pinet. Picpoul, the name of the grape, means lip-stinger, a reference to the wine's sharp flavour when it's first pressed; Pinet is a village a handful of kilometres from Marseillan. Light, crisp, citric, delicate and dangerously quaffable, Picpoul de Pinet goes down very pleasantly on a steamy summer night as you pick and slurp your way through a mound of shellfish. Which is always what we plan to eat whenever we visit the nearby coastal town of Sète.

From the Abbaye de Valmagne, the most direct route to this busy Mediterranean port is an inland road. But one blue and golden day in early autumn, we backtracked to Marseillan and took the long way to Sète via the flat, straight causeway that runs between the Etang de Thau and the sea. It was too gorgeous an afternoon not to stop for a while, and once we had made our way through a thin fringe of low scrubby plants we found ourselves on one of the finest beaches imaginable. The sand was fine as berry sugar and our bare feet broke through the crusty top layer dried by the sun. Pale blue near the shore, the water deepened to indigo on the horizon, its sound a basso profundo roar,

like standing under a waterfall, that peaked and ebbed as each
wave came in. Scattered along the beach were seashells striped in
butter yellows and deep toffee browns. A woman in a bikini
walked a trio of small dogs, one milk chocolate, one white chocolate, the third the hue of dark cocoa.

It was with some reluctance that
we climbed into the car and drove the
few remaining kilometres to Sète, a
charming miniature Venice with a maze
of intersecting canals. But don't be fooled
by the picturesque scenes; this is a serious port, its quay lined with fishing
boats and, on the horizon, the occasional glimpse of a cruiseliner or the
ferry that makes regular runs to Tangiers.

When it comes to tomatoes, apples
or just about any other ingredient, I believe that the closer it is
to where it grew up, the better it will taste. So in Sète, it was
unthinkable that we should eat anything other than fish. "Walk
to the end of the quay," advised the woman at the hotel when
we asked for restaurant suggestions. We did, past the lines of
fishing boats, past the open-air fish stall just closing up for the
day, its owner hosing it down, until we found a long string of
possibilities all advertising seafood. We promenaded back and
forth, assessing the menus on the boards outside, narrowing our
choice down to two and eventually picking La Calanque on the
basis of the vivacious crowd inside — and what we could see
on their plates.

Here, *moules frites* meant a mountain of mussels, a kilo apiece,
served in the large metal pot they had been steamed in, with a

smaller pot hooked on the side of the table for empty shells.
Oysters to start, Picpoul de Pinet to sip: the rest of the meal was
preordained. Meanwhile the table next to us, hosted, we con-
cluded, by the restaurant's owner, pulsed with high-energy
conversation. Hands semaphored, voices lifted, there was an
occasional outburst of song. We felt drawn into its circle of
bonhomie and left with a mutually cheery *"Bonsoir!"*

Sète has a number of culinary specialties, including *les zezettes
de Sète* — pastries the length of a man's hand, narrowing towards
each end — and the *tielle*, a small pie filled with octopus and
tomatoes whose rim of crimped pastry resembles the ropes that
lie along the quay. A comparative latecomer to Languedocien
cuisine, the *tielle* originated in Italy and was first commercialized in
1937 by a woman called Adrienne Verducci. Her granddaughter,
Josiane Cianni, has a stall in the market where she sells the pies
made by her brother Thierry.

You can also taste the intriguing pies called *pâtés de Pézenas*,
after a town midway between Béziers and Sète. Small and tall for
their size, like castle turrets — they'd be perfect
as pawns for an edible chessboard — they
are stuffed with a mixture of chopped
lamb and candied lemon. It's a bizarre
recipe that pays little heed to French

cuisine, which makes sense when you learn that the dish was invented for Lord Clive, the famous "Clive of India," who wintered near Pézenas for health reasons in 1768, bringing his native cook with him.

Meat of any kind seems an anomaly in Sète. I have rarely seen seafood in such profusion. *"Notre terre, c'est la mer,"* read a poetic poster for oysters in the indoor market. Below it were stiff-bodied mackerel, anchovies, octopus and dark spiny sea urchins, one opened to show off the five-pointed orange star of its edible gonads. At the shellfish stall, a woman arranged trays of mussels of various kinds. At twelve francs a kilo, *moules de Bouzigues* are the cheapest, she told me, and good for *moules marinières*, but saltier than the *moules de mer*, which cost a franc a kilo more. As their name implied, the much bigger, and costlier, *moules à farcir* ("mussels to stuff") had room enough for a fancy filling like the one we had tasted at La Table d'Emilie in Marseillan.

Oysters are at their best when there's an "r" in the month but you can eat mussels all year round and whenever we go to France, they are one of the first dishes I cook. More familiar with the smooth, unblemished shells of farmed mussels, I had always thought of them as a fast dish to prepare: rinse, check that they are all closed, into the pot, and supper was on the table. But things are more complicated in France. Whereas cleaning oysters is easy — the French even make a special oyster glove of stout rubber to protect your palm — cleaning mussels can be a lengthy process that involves scraping off numerous little white worm-like accretions and using sheer force to strip the mussels of their whiskery brown beards. I have learned to ignore the white worms and the barnacles, but on my first tries it took me twenty minutes to clean a kilo — and we can easily get through two kilos as a main course, accompanied, more often than not, by a bottle or two of Picpoul de Pinet.

Wine and shellfish are natural companions. The day we visited Domaine de la Baume near Béziers, talk over lunch turned to the various types of bivalves common along the Mediterranean coast. This recipe is adapted from one given me by Jérôme Girard, who was then the winemaker there.

MEDITERRANEAN MUSSELS

2	glasses of good white wine	2
1	onion, chopped	1
8	cloves garlic, chopped	8
	Parsley, thyme, tarragon, chives, bay leaf	
4 lbs	small mussels	2 kg
1 tbsp	butter	15 mL
1 tbsp	flour	15 mL
	Pepper to taste	
	Juice of half a lemon	

Cook wine, onion, garlic and herbs slowly together until onion and garlic are softened. Add the mussels, cover and cook until they open. Remove the mussels and keep warm. Reserve the juice.

Melt butter in a large pan and mix in the flour, stirring until smooth. Cook gently for two minutes, continuing to stir. Whisk in reserved mussel liquid and cook until thickened. Add pepper, lemon juice and mussels to sauce, and mix gently. Serve with plenty of bread to mop up the sauce.

Serves 4

CHAPTER 5

Wild Beef and Salt

THE CAMARGUE, AIGUES-MORTES AND NÎMES

One of the most bewitching films of my childhood was a story about the white horses of the Camargue. More recently, we had been entranced by another French movie, Latcho Drom, which told the history, in images and music, of the Roma as they spread across Europe. A modern sequence took audiences to the Camargue and the town where the gypsies gather each year to salute their saint. Sitting there in the movie theatre, I nudged Peter. "Let's go there next year."

Where the Rhône river trickles and spreads into the Mediterranean is a massive fan-shaped delta shaped like the roots of a tree, a vast triangle, enigmatic, eerie and utterly flat. On the map, the Camargue is a tattered lace of islets and ponds as though, on the day of creation, neither element would yield to the other. It is a place of extremes, of bulrushes that gleam like the pearly insides of oyster shells, flamingos of an almost neon pink and the largest, most vicious mosquitoes we had ever encountered.

The Camargue is also a larder, an area that brims with food. Its waters produce *salicorne* (the green vegetable that we had tasted near Béziers) and mountains of rice and salt; its sands grow a vine for a specific type of wine (*vin des sables*); and for meat, there are the black bulls with their lyre-shaped horns that roam free across this vast marshland.

A strange and alluring region unlike any other, the Camargue's scenery can be defined in a few brushstrokes: quill-like poplars on the horizon, wet pools shining like small mirrors amongst the marsh plants, a landscape of rivers and deltas in miniature. Even from a considerable distance you can spot the marble whiteness of the wild Camargue horses with their long, ground-sweeping tails. They are said to be the descendants of an Arabian steed abandoned in the Midi in the eighth century, our daughter Kate, an aficionado of anything equine, told us as we drove towards the sea.

The dearth of trees and the even plane of the land give the scenery a northern look: it could be the Netherlands or Norfolk, except for the flamingos and a sky that most days is an unbroken cerulean blue. Orchards flatten out into marshes of silver dotted with clumps of needle-like grass the virulent unreal green of Astroturf. Edging the ditches along the sides of the road, rushes dance and rustle in the wind. It is impractical to build on a sponge, so few roads cross the Camargue; the main highway leads south to Stes. Maries de la Mer, which is named for not one but three saints: Mary Magdalene, Mary Jacobé and, depending on which legend you believe, Mary Salomé or the Virgin Mary herself. All agree that this group, plus a serving girl called Sara, crossed the Mediterranean after the Crucifixion and landed on the south coast of France. In gratitude for their landfall, the three Marys built a small chapel, from which Christianity spread throughout western Europe. But it is the humble servant Sara who gives the seaside town much of its fame. For she is the patron saint of gypsies (stories differ as to why) and, on May 24 each year, when Christians assemble to hail the Marys, gypsies from all over Europe gather to salute their Sara.

We had left our rented cottage near Béziers behind and were on a short road trip, wanting to show Kate the Camargue's famous white horses and see the statue of Saint Sara for ourselves. On the way, it seemed appropriate to delve a little more into the history of the wandering peoples who so revered her. Poorly signposted from the main road and unprepossessing at first sight, the *Ecomusée Tzigane* (Gypsy Museum) was little more than half a dozen caravans standing at random in a parched field. But what better to represent these nomadic peoples, we thought as we piled out of the car, than their traditional mode of transport?

The museum goes to some length to educate the visitor on what gypsies are *not*. *Tziganes* are not the same as *voyageurs*, a sign explained. They could be Romany, Manouche, Suté, Kale or Gitanos, each of whom speak different dialects. With their lace curtains and rush-seated chairs, the caravans on display, most fifty to sixty years old, offered a rare look at the nomadic way of life, which seemed to offer an ideal combination of homey comfort and total mobility.

A display listed famous gypsies, including the Gypsy Kings musical group, whose members originated nearby, and jazz guitarist Django Reinhardt. Another board tracked the peoples' progress, from India, which they left in the tenth century, through Greece and on to Western Europe. Their arrival was followed by two centuries of persecution, which finally ended, officially at least, in 1783, when Charles III declared *les gitans* equal to other citizens. In 1852 comes the first mention of "Bohemians" in Stes. Maries de la Mer.

On Saint Sara's day, colourful caravans cram the streets of the little seaside town of Stes. Maries de la Mer and as many people as possible crowd into the church. There they tenderly remove the statue of their saint and bear her through the town and across the beach to the sea, where they immerse her in the water. But on the hot and dazzling June day of our visit, the road into the town was free of traffic and most visitors were outside, basking on the sand or strolling along the seafront promenade licking ice cream cones. The sturdy twelfth-century church was almost empty. A wall of heat met us as we descended a stone stairway into the low arched crypt where racks held hundreds of candles lit to Saint Sara: tall tapered ones, stubby white ones and small votives in red glass holders. Soot had completely blackened the ceiling. It was a homely space and the diminutive brown-faced statue draped in robes seemed a friendly little figure. The chapel is Sara's alone. The three Marys have the main part of the church, where a wall niche holds a polychrome statue of two of them, doll-like figures in pink and blue robes, afloat in a small boat with the third, presumably the Virgin Mary, looking down from a painting above.

Back on the seafront, it was obvious something was happening — families were abandoning the beach, scrabbling their towels and picnic baskets together and hurrying their offspring along. Nudging and teasing each other, groups of young men flowed in from the side streets. In our experience, following a southern French crowd, even if there isn't a market in sight, invariably leads to serendipitous discoveries: a street dance, a wedding, a festival. This time it was a bullfight. While blood is spilled in arenas elsewhere, the *corridas* of the Camargue place man and beast on an equal footing; the contest does not end in death. Prices were chalked on the wall outside, about the cost of a movie, so we joined the queue and handed our money in through a slot-like window to the invisible someone within.

Inside the arena, which holds about 3,500, the seats were numbered in white paint, and a jeans-clad crew was hosing down the oval of sand. A gaggle of boys clustered around the gate where the bulls would enter. From off-stage came a cacophony of trumpets, tambourine and drum. Voices bounced around the steadily filling stadium as the audience streamed in: couples fresh off the beach, some still in swimsuits; old folk; teenagers; a tiny girl in a blue-banded straw boater. A man in front of us leafed through a paleontology textbook while all around, spectators who had finished with their morning newspapers folded them into sun hats. A woman walked up and down the steps between the rows of seats selling cellophane-wrapped packages of popcorn and potato chips, and throats bulged as people swigged from pale blue bottles of Volvic water.

The band struck up. The woman sitting next to Peter beat time with her sandalled foot, her hair a long black streamer, her Provençal skirt a froth of frills, her cat's-eye sunglasses pure

Hollywood. The anticipation was tangible. Finally, to the tune of — no surprise this — the "Toreador's Song" from *Carmen*, five young *razeteurs*, clad in pure white down to their running shoes, marched into the arena.

The name *razeteur* comes from *razet*, the small comb which the Camargue bullfighter uses to retrieve a rosette from between the bull's horns, or tassels attached to them. Neither cruel nor bloody, it was more like a game of tag, although some bulls didn't seem keen on playing. The first animal lumbered around lethargically until whistles and shouts from the crowd eventually prompted a single half-hearted charge. The second bull banged his head on the gate as he entered the arena, not an auspicious start, then stood stock still like a cross headmaster regarding a classroom of rambunctious schoolboys. Having gained everyone's full attention, he ran into the arena and came to a halt. If there had been grass, he would have grazed. To distract the audience from the lack of action, a tinny voice promoted a local disco over the public address system.

Bull Number Three more than made up for his predecessors. Downright vicious, he knew all the crowd-pleasing tricks, pawing the ground, then retreating with ominous slowness as we held our collective breaths. Then he attacked, from zero to sixty in seconds, almost clambering over the wooden barrier separating him from the audience. But there was little real danger, only plenty of thrills as the *razeteurs* skillfully ricocheted off or vaulted the boards. Events sometimes swerved perilously close to farce: at one point, a small bird landed in the arena steps away from a bull and pecked around in the sand in search of insects. Some bouts were slow and inconclusive, others fast and heart-stopping, especially when a bull hooked the topmost board of the barrier and tossed it into the air. We stayed till the end of the very last confrontation, having experienced plenty of drama but no death, no blood in the sand or bits of animal anatomy distributed to the favoured. The ending was anticlimactic, but in a good way; we left knowing that no bulls had been harmed and that, the event over, they would be returned to their wild, marshy home. Till the next time.

Our next time came a year later, in much cooler weather. Travelling without Kate this time, we paid our usual respects to Saint Sara, then headed north to Nîmes. Once a Roman settlement, the largest town in the Camargue still has plenty of well-preserved evidence of how those conquerors lived almost two thousand years ago. Art students from a nearby school perch on the ledges of a grave square building called the Maison Carrée which, with its imperial flight of steps, impressive columns and friezes, looks like the temple it originally was before functioning as, among other things, a stable and church. A massive stone gate, *la porte d'Auguste*, has separate openings for pedestrians and chariots. Most evocative of all is *les arènes*, a full-size Roman amphitheatre still in operation.

Determined to stay as close to it as possible, we grabbed a map from the Nîmes tourist office, strolled a few blocks and spotted a hotel directly across the street from the colossal stone edifice. Off to do her afternoon shopping, Madame gave us keys to two rooms; "Whichever you want," she said. The decision was instant. The room on the first floor was smaller than the other one but the view — a section of the arena's massive stone arches, floodlit at night — filled the window frame to the exclusion of all else. The stone was a sullen grey in the early morning, as we would learn later when we sat up in bed.

The arena is a year-round venue. That afternoon we watched workmen, reduced to the size of ants within the huge oval, busy installing the inflatable superstructure that allows it to be used throughout the winter. This protection from the weather was not a modern innovation: holes around the uppermost tier, one hundred and twenty of them, once held masts to support enormous sails, controlled by ropes and pulleys, that kept the rain off as many as 23,000 spectators below. They were here to watch man fight man or man fight bulls, dogs or wild boar. Nothing more savage than that on the gladiatorial playbill, said the guide who was showing a group of us around, because the protective barrier was not high enough to keep lions or tigers from attacking those in the prime seats. Performances were free, she added — given the proverbial bread and circuses, the populace was happy.

Getting a grasp on how long a building this ancient has stood is like trying to comprehend that space goes on and on into infinity. Around this colossal stone oval, dwellings had risen and fallen, every paving stone had been stepped on uncountable times, and innumerable hands had touched the walls we were touching now. To put it in perspective, the arena's beginnings were twice as remote in time to medieval Languedociens as medieval castles are to us. Nineteen centuries after it was built, it is still a formidably intelligent piece of design with an intricate system of stairways and tunnels that quickly diverted the aristocracy and the lower classes to their appropriate seating sections and, when the show was over, emptied the stadium within ten minutes. As we climbed to the uppermost tiers, the guide indicated the faint grooves in the stone that defined individual seating spaces, a carefully measured forty centimetres apart, a tight fit for some of today's generous bottoms.

The arena has a lively history that has seen it evolve from entertainment site to fortress to a village with two hundred homes, two churches and as many as 2,000 residents. Cleaned out and restored in the late 1700s, it is now a venue for bullfights, tennis games, ice shows and concerts. Rock concerts, I hope; I like to think of the seats filled with thousands of kids, most wearing denim, more than a few of them smokers, and only a handful aware that they are rocking in the hometown of blue jeans and cigarettes.

Nîmes was the birthplace of a uniquely misguided French ambassador. Sent to Portugal in the mid-sixteenth century, Jean Nicot heard from a friend about the healing powers of tobacco. When an experiment on an ailing acquaintance convinced him first-hand of its qualities, Nicot not only planted cuttings in the French Embassy gardens but also sent tobacco plants to the French court and snuff to Catherine de Medici as a migraine medicine. It must have worked. At any rate, she was sufficiently impressed to decree that tobacco should be named Herba Regina: "the queen's herb." Nicot's own name, however, would last longer. The tobacco plant was eventually called *Nicotiana tabacum* and the substance it contained became known as nicotine.

It's a dubious claim to fame that the city doesn't make much of, and it's far outweighed by Nîmes being the original source of today's most popular fabric. Nobody knows precisely how far back denim's distinctive weave goes — work clothing tends to get worn to rags and rarely ends up in museums — but the Musée de Vieux Nîmes contains a child's jacket from the nineteenth century which, if you examine it close up, shows the irregular weave of indigo blue and white threads unique to denim. Known simply as *serge de Nîmes*, the durable fabric was originally made into everyday clothing for farmers and labourers. Then in 1860, a European immigrant to the United States named Lévi-Strauss cut the *serge* into comfortable trousers, riveted for strength; the name was soon shortened to *de Nîmes* or just "denim." Before they became popularized as icons of rebellion, denim jeans were worn by the cowboys of the Wild West, whose cattle, like the fighting bulls of Roman times and the wild bulls of the Camargue, all eventually ended up on the table.

All around the Camargue, the meat of the local bulls is prized for its forthright flavour. We had noticed *carpaccio de toro* on a menu in Stes. Maries de la Mer, but in most restaurants the bull went straight into the cooking pot to be served up as *boeuf à la gardiane*, said to be the favourite dish of *gardians*, the men who tend Camargue bulls. If they could eat bull, why not us? Didn't an afternoon of energetic sightseeing consume as many calories as babysitting a few torpid cattle?

Early that evening we left our hotel across from the arena and made our way up a side street into a little square. A huge palm tree like a gigantic dishmop stood at its centre and a crocodile sculpture skulked at the base of a fountain (Nîmes was founded by Roman soldiers who had fought and beaten Cleopatra's — or rather her lover, Antony's — army in Egypt; as a reminder of the conquest, the city's coat of arms shows a crocodile chained to a palm tree.) Merrily painted in yellow, turquoise and the colour of ripe cantaloupe, a bistro, Le P'tit Nîmois, offered *mer* or *terre*, surf or turf: a cassoulet of monkfish, langoustines and mussels or the decidedly earthy beef specialty of the region. Whether from a Camarguais *toro* or not, the huge chunks of meat were dark with the long fibres that reveal a hardworking muscle selected for flavour. Leisurely braising had rendered the meat tender as butter, the black olives integral to the dish contributed a lusty undernote, and there was a large heap of Camarguais rice to soak up the sauce.

But had I really tasted authentic wild bull meat — or was it just beef? Some of the butchers' stalls at Nîmes' indoor market were closed the following morning and, frustratingly, I couldn't locate anyone who could tell me. Sometimes I don't find what I am after but, call it serendipity, I almost always make some other, often completely unrelated, discovery. Empty basket, open mind. This time it was *tellines*, tiny amber and grey shellfish from the Mediterranean whose resemblance to surf-tumbled beach pebbles was remarkable.

"What do you do with them?" I asked the man at the fish stall. (Not "what does one do, namely me," but "what do *you* do?," a reliable way of procuring authentic home-cooked recipes.)

Cook them with garlic and parsley, he said. Meanwhile his wife scooped up a heap of mussels with the clattering sound of stones caught in the undertow and shoveled them onto the scale. There were *palourdes* here too, clams striped russet, honey and cream, some patterned like herringbone; the same ones, I suspected, that we had seen on the beach south of Sète.

Shellfish abound around here, and not just at the markets. I thought of the giant clamshell and the Titan statue in Béziers. Just inside the entrance to Nîmes cathedral are two matching greyish-white fonts, deeply ridged and ribbed, attached to opposite walls; they are halves of a gargantuan shell, the hinge like the cochlea of a giant. Easily large enough for the simultaneous baptism by total immersion of unusually hefty twins, each basin is at least a metre long. I was more curious about edible than religious possibilities. What would you do with a shellfish this large? Steam it? Cut it in steaks, beat it on the rocks to tenderize it and fricassee it? I couldn't help wondering whether the meat had been chewy or tender, and how many people this colossal mollusc had fed.

Where there is seawater, there is salt. But when the waters are too saline, life cannot exist: as at Aigues-Mortes, literally "dead waters," a town in the western Camargue some forty kilometres from Nîmes. Facing onto the marshes where salt is gathered and packaged — much of it in the tall blue cylinders with the whale logo that have become a feature in trendy restaurants around the globe — Aigues-Mortes is a sturdy *bastide* town with uncompromising stone walls and numerous watchtowers framing its lattice of streets, not as fairy-tale as Carcassonne but just as engaging in its own way. Walking through a sturdy gateway brought us into the bustling Grande Rue Jean Jaurès, which led us in turn into a generously proportioned square at whose centre stood a statue of King Louis IX. The town was founded by Louis in 1240 as a port, a gateway to prosperous trade with Italy and the Orient. From here he left for the crusades and became known as Saint Louis. His castle no longer exists but a massive tower that he built does, and it was from here, the next morning, that we began a leisurely stroll along the ramparts of the old town, the work of Louis' successors, the beguilingly named Philippe the Bold and Philippe the Fair. Shifting sands put an end to its days as a port, a role taken over by Marseille.

A walk right around the giant square of the ramparts gave us a seagull's view of the town, of well-worn leather boots placed out to dry on a windowsill, of hidden courtyards and laundry lines strung with towels and of quilted red rooftops and skylights winking in the sun. On the eaves of a shed, an ebony cat snoozed among a tumble of crimson-leaved Virginia creeper. In small, secluded gardens, tables were already set for lunch. Below us, in the tidy narrow streets, artists' galleries and every-day commerce thrived side by side.

If Carcassonne is fantasy, Aigues-Mortes is function; comparing them is like comparing a peacock to a thrush. But in their own way, Aigues-Mortes' walls were just as evocative of the past. With my eyes half shut, it didn't take much imagination to picture the sentinels of centuries ago patrolling back and forth, constantly on the alert for a sudden movement or glint of light between the battlements or through the small square apertures that punctuated the walls. They must have been exposed to the elements and bitterly cold, but when their watch was over they could retreat to the domesticity of the tower rooms threaded along the ramparts, to warm their hands at the hefty fireplaces and rest a while on the built-in stone benches that flanked the windows, like seats in a train compartment.

We had now walked along one full side of the square ramparts. Turning the corner revealed a vista of open countryside: a field with two white horses and, far beyond, the *camelles*, impossibly massive, gleaming white banks of salt harvested from the sea water. The Camargue's relentless sun and two great winds, the Mistral from the east and the Tramontane from the west, all help in the evaporation process that leaves the salt behind.

Two more sides of the square, another corner and several more tower rooms, and we were back at Louis' Constance Tower. Climbing the stairway to the top opened up a 360-degree view that took in the salt marshes to the south and, to the north, the canal that begins in Sète, skirts the Camargue and heads north across the countryside to the town of Beaucaire on the Rhône. Another voyage to ponder.

Aigues-Mortes seemed like a good place to taste the *tellines* we had noticed in the market at Nîmes. Today, almost every café in the square listed them on the lunch menu. Those I ordered were simply cooked with parsley and a head-spinning lashing of garlic — pretty much as the fishmonger in Nîmes market had recommended — and heaped in a bowl, with oak-leaf lettuce on the side. In terms of hard work, *tellines* make the dismantling of an artichoke look like fast food. None is much larger than a thumbnail and a fork is useless; fiddling the sweet, briny meat out with your teeth and fingers is the easiest way to get at it. "How many are there in a serving?" asked Peter, already two-thirds of the way though his goat cheese and salad. With Saint Louis looking down, I nested the shells in tens, like stacks of tiny open books, as I emptied them, but gave up when I reached a hundred. Even with plenty of bread to sop up the salty juices, they made a barely adequate lunch.

Lettuce   chevre chaud   tomato   white onion slices   black olives   vinaigrette on side   green olives   noix walnuts   chevre chaud   on toasted baguette

There are worse views to wake up to than old weathered stone. Set just inside the city walls, our hotel room looked directly across at the ramparts. A popular place, the hotel's restaurant was already filling up with large groups by early evening. In the mood for somewhere quieter, we strolled back in the vague direction of the square along a side street which led us to a pink building with shutters the green of fresh almonds and wisteria and clematis clambering over a painted green trellis. L'Oustau Camarguais promised regional cooking — witness the bull on the wrought-iron sign outside — and that night's *table d'hôte* menu included both *tellines* and *gardiane de toro*. Inside, the restaurant had yellow-washed walls, tempting aromas wafting from the kitchen and the sense that behind and above, family life went on. The salty-sweet *tellines* were cloaked in a warm sauce. Madame beamed when I asked her what went into it. Wine, cream, shallots and garlic. The bull meat in the *gardiane*, she said, sat overnight in a bath of red wine (possibly the local Costières de Nîmes, that went down so well with it). The chef, while he did not include the usual black olives, did, she admitted, add "secret" ingredients: orange peel, fennel and a touch of caramel. It was dark, earthy and good, and for dessert there was a clafoutis studded with tiny cubes of pumpkin, its surface cross-hatched with raspberry coulis, and a lemony *crème catalane* whose fire-hardened caramel crust cracked like thin ice on a frosty day.

A shop on the main street — another rue Jean Jaurès, in fact, Grande Rue Jean Jaurès, to add to the collection — had a window filled with packages of salt, bottles of local wine and *toro à la gardiane*, both in a rectangular steel pan and in big glistening jars, the contents produced, the label read, on a local farm. I went inside to find out how it was made here. "Marinate it overnight in a bottle of *vin des sables* [the local wine], carrots, onions and thyme," said the butcher, Bernard Sabdes. "Cook it all morning, with olives and a bouquet garni. Eat it with rice from the Camargue." Simple.

This Camarguais dish is comfort food for winter weekends. Saturday afternoon I mix up the marinade. Sometime Sunday I do the cooking, then gently reheat it at suppertime and serve it with rice, mashed potatoes, or noodles.

BOEUF À LA GARDIANE

3 lbs	stewing beef, cut into 1-inch (2.5-cm) cubes	1 1/2 kg
2 cups	sturdy red wine	500 mL
4	cloves garlic	4
2	large onions, sliced	2
2	carrots, sliced	2
1 tsp	thyme	5 mL
1 tsp	rosemary	5 mL
1	bay leaf	1
1/4 cup	olive oil	60 mL
2/3 cup	black olives, pitted	170 mL

Mix all ingredients together except olive oil and olives and marinate overnight.

The following day, remove the beef and dry the cubes with a paper towel. Reserve the marinade.

In a large frypan or casserole dish, heat the olive oil and brown cubes on all sides. Add herbs, marinade and olives. Cover and simmer at low heat for 2 hours or until beef is fork-tender.

Serves 6

Tiny clams stand in for tellines in this starter dish.

CLAMS WITH CREAM

4 tbsp	butter	60 mL
3	garlic cloves, finely chopped	3
2/3 cup	white wine	170 mL
2 lb	small clams	1 kg
1/2 cup	whipping cream	125 mL
1/4 cup	chopped parsley	60 mL

Melt butter, add garlic and cook over low-medium heat until the garlic starts to soften. Add wine. Add clams and cover. Cook until all are open. Drain clams, reserving the liquid, and keep warm. Boil until reduced by half, whisk in cream and simmer until sauce thickens, pour over clams and sprinkle with chopped parsley.

Serves 4 as a starter

CHAPTER 6

Cheese, Cheese and Cheese

MONTPELLIER

Monday morning in Mirepoix. Market day in the town that's just a ten-minute drive from the village where we now live part of the year. Peter is intent on drawing a stall laden with plaits of garlic. I have tonight's supper to buy. "See you in the café." He finishes early and when we meet, not only is my basket full but he's juggling a half-dozen plastic bags. Did I see that woman with the goat cheese? I bought two. So, it turns out, did he — and he's also paid a visit to the red-bereted man with the cheese truck. On our way back home, as always, we stop at the SuperU supermarket for bottled water and, as usual, can't resist a swing by the cheese section. Goat cheese, fresh, aged and rolled in herbs; cheese made with cow's and sheep's milk: so far our personal best is fourteen varieties on the go at the same time.

On our second and on all subsequent visits to the Languedoc, we rented small houses in various villages, temporary homes that provided space to spread out and, more to the point, room to cook. Jet lag doesn't matter; our first stop en route from the airport is always for edibles. We stock up on basics: salt, olive oil, vinegar. We buy pastis and wine, sliced ham for tomorrow's lunch, a can of duck confit and a bar or two of our favourite French chocolate, the Poulain brand 200-gram bar of *Lait noisettes au feuilleté de praliné*, dense with little crispy chunks of praline and whole hazelnuts. And, invariably, we overindulge ourselves at the cheese counter.

The *fromage* collection grows as the days go by: little round Picodons from the Ardèche made of goat's milk (the name means "spicy" in Occitan); Pélardons, similar in shape and size, from the Cévennes mountains north of Montpellier; and other *cabécous* (Occitan for "little goat's cheese"), like the diminutive Rocamadour. We eat sheep's milk cheeses too, the Brébis from the slopes of the Pyrenees where flocks have grazed for over two thousand years. With just two of us eating, we accumulate and accumulate cheeses in varying stages of ripeness, including the pale, semi-firm Ariègeois, an addictive and assertive variety that I've never been able to find outside its region.

The Languedoc's most distinguished *fromage*, a wedge of ink-scribbled ivory, a celestial fusion of cream and salt on the tongue, comes from Roquefort-sur-Soulzon, a village northwest of Montpellier. A visit was called for, although, to be honest, I was more excited by the prospect of forming a closer acquaintance with Montpellier, a place we had already found engaging on a brief, accidental visit in 1993.

Journeying across the south, we had planned to drive around the city but were drawn into its spell, spun in on a silvery highway that led to its heart. As we tried to untangle ourselves, sweaty, irritable and tired, fate made a hotel sign appear.

"Enough of this, let's see if they have a room," said Peter.

Unpacked, cleaned up and in a much better frame of mind, we walked over to the old town and came upon more magic. Bridging the streets were lengths of rope hung with bundles of greenery: clippings of olive, box, pine, thyme and bay, identified by handwritten labels in French and Latin, in celebration of the Botanical Gardens' four-hundredth anniversary.

Repeated trips have convinced me that Montpellier, population 225,000, is as near as it comes to the perfect city, a felicitous mix of the imposing and the intimate, its startling modern architecture juxtaposed with an alluring web of ancient alleys and squares. It has both grave and handsome churches and the optimistic, youthful air of a thriving university town. The Botanical Gardens, the first in Europe, were founded in 1593 as an educational resource for students at the nearby medical school. Today they are as much pleasure gardens as teaching aids, with stone benches to sit on and terra cotta urns spilling bright pink fuchsias. As well as lavenders and dark blue spikes of hyssop, the medicinal plant section contains rosemary, thyme and mints of all kinds. One time there, I remember rubbing a leaf of lemon balm between my fingers and being surprised by the intensity of its fragrance. Australia's flourishing wine industry began with vines shipped from these gardens in the 1830s.

Gravel paths ran between five vegetable beds shaped like picture frames, one inside the other, bursting with peppers, onions, red orach, rhubarb, tomatoes, dill and sage, orange and yellow calendulas and artichokes. Strawberries ripened in the shadow of a tree whose cherries were so tautly plump with juice that each one bore a gleaming white highlight. Pausing in her leisurely raking of a path, a gardener pointed out nasturtiums and all manner of cucumbers twining up bamboo trellises. Even in early summer, she was already deeply tanned; certainly, she concurred, on a day like this, her job was more than agreeable.

From garden to market is one small step and — one more reason why I like it — Montpellier is rich in markets, including the modern Halles Laissac, which is circular and built of concrete but still hides culinary treasures. Today, the produce stall displayed purple-striped garlic from the Tarn and *haricots rouges*, their pods a deep cochineal pink streaked with creamy green, like a dress for a garden party. Next to them were perfectly round courgettes and *rougette* lettuces, their dark green leaves stained a hectic red like the cheeks of a doomed Victorian heroine. This was also artichoke heaven. I noticed the globe-shaped Macau variety and another type wider than it was high, and yet another kind, its leaves folded outwards like a flower's petals.

Near the artichokes was an avalanche of almonds. Freshly picked, the nuts are a gentle green and slightly fuzzy, like very expensive suede or the fur of a dormouse. "What do you do with them?" I asked the man at the stall. In reply, he pulled a knife from his pocket, cut the almond in half, scooped out the soft white kernel and offered it to me. It was sweet and refreshing, its almond flavour just beginning to emerge. One aisle over, at the butcher's stall, was proof that coating anything in rosy-gold aspic makes it look delicious, just as so many words sound better in French. *Couennes, oreilles, langue* and *jarret* made a poem of love, but in English meant rolls of pork skin, ears, tongue and knuckle.

All this abundance was driving me to distraction. Because we were on the first stage of a road trip and staying in hotels, we wouldn't be able to cook for ourselves for several days. It was a bittersweet experience roaming around the Halles Castellane, a large indoor market in the Old Quarter close by yet another Place Jean Jaurès. Arriving at the *crémerie*, all I could do was imagine a long Sunday lunch with cheese served after roast chicken (and before wedges of the ripe, drippy, greeny-gold Charentais melon at the stand nearby, whose lush scent made me want to bite into one there and then). For six people, stallholder Michelle Farman suggested a total of 300 grams of cheese: "Le Roquefort, le Cantal and one or two *chèvres*." She itemized her recommendations on fingertips painted the same scarlet as the overalls that set off her silvery hair so effectively.

Madame Farman sold honey too. The clear, golden honey *de tilleul* came from the same linden flowers that make such an excellent tisane. The soft, creamy *toutes fleurs* was as yellow and opaque as lemon curd. The *châtaignier* was a jar of dissolved amber and tasted assertively of its chestnut origins. The honeys made from Provençal lavender and rosemary from the Montagne de la Clape near Narbonne were both creamy and thick, the colour of cottage walls. *Miel de garrigues* was opaque, as dark as resin, aromatic from the thyme and other herbs that the bees

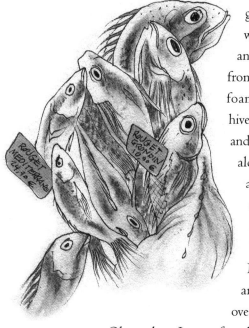

graze on. *Miel d'acacia*, the lightest, was clear, blonde and runny — and don't forget to taste the honey from the Cévennes, where the ground foams with white heather and the hives are as much as 1500 metres high, and an aperitif called Hydromiel, an alcoholic fist in a slyly sweet glove, and a honey vinegar that you can add to vinaigrette or use to deglaze a pan in which you've browned chicken. And of course, continued Madame Farman, there's honey and cheese. Fresh honey drizzled over cloud-white fromage frais.

Oh my, how I yearn for a kitchen of my own when I go to a French market. Lettuces beg to be taken home, rinsed and anointed with olive oil. Apricots cry out to be stacked into a pyramid on a footed glass stand. If few occupations delight you more than making a meal, any Languedoc market is joy of a cruel kind. Renting a place for a few weeks altered the way we ate. As well as croissants and *pains aux chocolat* from the *boulangerie*, I might buy a fresh baguette, then slather it with sweet butter and strawberry jam. More bread, sometimes the second baguette of the day, accompanied lunch which we ate outside as long as the weather smiled on us, in the garden or on the terrace beside the row of tumbling scarlet geraniums that came with our temporary home.

Cheese, charcuterie, a plate of sliced tomatoes sprinkled with sea salt and olive oil; lunch was never complex. If our day took us into the countryside or near the sea, we'd pack a picnic

— basically the same foods, except for the tomatoes, which we did not slice but bit into like apples, nibbling small holes in their skins and sucking out the warm, sweetly acidic interiors.

If lunch meant a café, we assiduously read the outdoor blackboards, seeking a place that served whatever was local, fresh and in season, like the *tellines* in Aigues-Mortes. In Montpellier, we came on a restaurant whose owner's values were exactly the same as ours: Le Ban des Gourmands, a convivial little place on a neighbourly square near the railway station. The dining room was long and wedge-shaped, with rush-seated chairs tucked under a dozen tables set with soft blue fruit-patterned linen. Chalked on a large board, a replica of the one outside on the pavement, the menu was carried from table to table. From the kitchen came the rasping sound of a knife slicing fresh crusty bread.

Cuisine du marché means exactly what it says: a menu that hinges on whatever the chef finds as he shops. A former Parisian who moved south because of the sun, chef Jacques Delepine roamed the market each morning in quest of what was fresh. That day he had found fillets of perch, which he had bathed in a mixture of lemon juice and olive oil seasoned with coriander, Szechuan pepper and salt from the Camargue. Two hours of marinating for the fish; a half hour for its salad of shredded zucchini. It was a disarming dish, totally refreshing, and suddenly breast of veal with morels did not seem out of the question or, if we paced ourselves carefully, the cherry clafoutis that followed. Yet again, the concept of the two-hour lunch made eminent sense.

When it comes to cheese, Delepine likes to set out Coulommiers, Reblochon, cheese from Corsica (where his wife comes from) and other varieties, all of which he buys from

Fromagerie Georges Bou in the Halles Castellane. We were there early next morning. The dark-haired Monsieur Bou has been minding the stall since 1982, his mother, born ten kilometres from Roquefort, since 1934. Under the slanting glass top of his display case, he had set out his cheeses on mats of straw: little bricks of Saint Nicolas, a raw milk goat's cheese; Pont L'Evêque in its square wooden box; *bleu des causses*; Munster from Alsace; Roquefort; and Pélardon from the Cévennes, so fresh that it seemed to be only one minor step beyond solidified cream. Those are only two days old, Monsieur Bou told us: "Eat them with sugar for dessert." The ones next to them were twelve days old, and thus ideal for putting on toast to go on a salad. Up on the counter, propped in a basket, was a magazine article. "*No*, raw milk cheeses won't kill you," insisted the headline. Georges Bou agreed completely: "The taste is the difference." It's like comparing a real chicken that has fed and scratched in the barn-yard to *poulets industriels*, battery hens. *The taste is the difference.* The diluted and suspect flavour of the factory-produced versus the real, the *authentique*.

Later that morning, as we wandered through Montpellier's Old Quarter, church bells batted the air, sending flocks of swifts flying like dust motes. This is no logical *bastide* town, and streets bend and curve confusingly. As we paused in a square to get our bearings, sounds drifted down from windows. Underlying the delicate geometry of a Bach partita on a faintly heard piano was another, more muscular piano, most definitely *forte*, constructing arpeggios like a series of steps for a school class to climb with their voices. Nearer the cathedral of Saint-Pierre, ribbons of music — flute, violin, a bassoon — unwound from different directions and entwined themselves in mid-air.

Protecting the entrance to the cathedral is a high stone canopy supported by two cone-topped columns like fat sharpened pencils. Beneath it, confetti from a recent wedding swirled, coins of tissue paper in orange, red, green and a turquoise as blue as the sea on a clear day. Most had moored themselves on the cobblestones, anchored there by a previous shower, fragments from a pointillist painting. Inside, a bee-like murmur of prayer and a stream of communicants returning down the aisle indicated mass was nearing its conclusion. As we stood at the rear of the cathedral, the organ sounded abruptly just behind us, a single huge majestic chord that skewered us to the ground. This was sound you could hear through your *feet*. Carrying candles, white-robed choristers progressed up the aisle towards us, then turned and bowed to an ecclesiastic, magnificent in red and gold robes.

Montpellier is a city of imposing constructions, and few are more striking than the Place Royale du Peyrou, a vast promenade built in 1688. It was not hard to imagine the people of the town taking a turn in frock coats and periwigs along this wide corridor walled with plane trees, a grand *allée* that concludes with steps to what looks like a small Arcadian temple but is, somewhat prosaically, a water tower that marks the end of a spectacular double-arched aqueduct eight hundred metres long. Walking around, we were intrigued by what you could *not* do in Montpellier's green spaces: "Access is forbidden to people suspected, through their actions, of troubling the tranquility," went my gauche translation of the official signage. I looked at the boys playing an impromptu game of soccer and townspeople strolling arm in arm. This was indeed a place of untroubled tranquility.

According to our map Montpellier's river, the Lez, was some distance from the old town, but the afternoon was pleasant so we decided to walk there. The first stage, past construction sites, concrete mixers and a listless *boules* game, was charmless. Then the road cut abruptly through an archway between two modern apartment buildings, their stark lines softened by balconies merry with laundry, and we came to the river. Paved either side with concrete, it had the man-made look of a canal. But what transfixed us was the edifice on its far bank, a remarkable structure that glittered like an *arc de triomphe* faced with mirrors or some extraterrestrial sequined monument left by a spaceship. Facing it on our side of the river was an immense semicircle of six-storey buildings, a hybrid of Georgian crescent and Greek temple. Glimpsed far away, through the gap at their centre, was an arch crowned with a dome. We felt we had been transported to a different planet, but it was merely Antigone, the understandably controversial *quartier* designed in 1980 by Catalan architect Ricardo Bofill.

We walked towards the semicircle. Broad *allées* led between the neoclassical beige buildings, all on a scale that reduced humans to insect-like proportions, and eventually we found ourselves in a huge square. "Weird, *weird*," I wrote in my notebook, looking up at the postmodern curves and broken capitals. But the plane trees added a touch of familiarity, and beneath them old ladies in black sunned themselves on the benches and children played. Once the fountain at the centre was completed, you could see how this would become a village square, albeit a disconcertingly modern one. The greenery would flourish and, eventually, Antigone would simply look like a structure from science fiction outpaced by nature.

Somehow even the most modern architecture in France becomes humanized. I thought of the strings of jeans and underwear hung out to dry on the balconies of apartment towers, *défendu* in any North American city. Far from being squalid, the multi-coloured laundry looked cheery and turned what could have been just one more filing cabinet for humans into a place where people obviously lived. Even new houses here spoke the same traditional design language of terra cotta tiles, cream stucco and shutters. They lived amiably in their landscape, the right size for their lots, not overblown monsters squeezed as tightly together as subway commuters.

The long, arrow-straight path we had followed from the river eventually ended at an escalator that fed us into a conventional shopping centre. All stylish clothes and electronic equipment, it formed the bulwark between Antigone's unconventional modernity and the antiquity of the Place de la Comédie, the social heart of Montpellier. Spacious, energetic and undeniably attractive, it is lined with imposing pale buildings, all cupolas,

domes, stone heads and caryatids, with a handsome theatre
like a miniature Paris Opera and a moss-covered fountain of
the Three Graces at one end and a park at the other. Known
affectionately as *l'oeuf* — the egg — or the "O," the *Place* is
the city's living room where *le tout Montpellier* gathers.

So do we, whenever we come to the city, often in the hour
before dinner or for a sit-down after a walk, settling in at one of
the many cafés set around its perimeter. Overhead rectangular
umbrellas, dovetailed together, form an unbroken canopy, their
colours — off-white, lettuce green, flower-pot red and Gauloise-
packet blue — denoting where one restaurant ends and the neighbouring establishment begins. We like going there best late in the
day when a low-slung sun transforms glasses of grenadine and
mint *sirops* into rectangular jewels that glow like a caliph's gems,
pernod becomes milky moonstone and even beer, even an everyday *pression*, becomes for a moment a column of antique gold.

Sitting in that mindless state induced by a strenuous afternoon of exploring, I often think that the wedge-shaped, ivory-
coloured buildings that nose into the Place de la Comédie, their
tall windows embellished with ornate balconies, resemble the
prows of great ocean liners, and it does not seem impossible that
one, and then all, of these structures might break loose from
their moorings. I can picture them, flotillas of stately vessels
cruising the wide boulevards by the light of the moon, their fili-
gree decks lined with spectral passengers.

A front-row seat in a café in the Place de la Comédie offers
up hours of entertainment watching the antics of small boys
with remote-controlled cars, riders of motorized bikes shred-
ding the early evening calm, and rollerbladers running calculated
rings around pigeons. From time to time a sleek sky-blue tram

painted with white swallows glides across the square and disappears down a side street. Cars are forbidden in the Place, so when a small wayward Renault realizes its mistake, like a farcical character who sees he is in the wrong bedroom, it frantically reverses and speeds off. On the steps of the theatre, like a chorus line awaiting their cue, a shabby band of latter-day wanderers, hair in dreadlocks, backpacks at their feet, sit with their equally ramshackle dogs and half-heartedly beg money from passersby.

Our scheduled three days in Montpellier was drawing to a close. What should we do tomorrow? Roquefort, only a few hours' drive away, was nagging at us. The distance was small, but what would we actually see when we got there? Milking machines? Cheese lying mouldering on shelves? We idled through the small outdoor market at the end of the Place de la Comédie, noting apricots as orange as carrots and *fouace de l'Aveyron*, a loaf glistening with sugar grains the size of hailstones. Montpellier seemed obsessed with food, in a pleasant way. A cut-rate store — "everything 10 francs" — sold a CD-ROM on cuisines of the world. The *Midi Libre* runs a daily recipe on its back page and when a customer went berserk one evening in a café, the headline read, "He stabbed himself in front of his plate of charcuterie."

Time was waning: we had to be back at our cottage in a couple of days to meet friends who were passing through. It had come down to an either–or situation. Either we drove to Roquefort the following day or we treated ourselves to lunch at Le Jardin des Sens, then Montpellier's (indeed the Languedoc's) only three-star Michelin restaurant — it's since lost a star — before driving home. Neither Peter nor I is a gastronomic scalp-collector, but neither had we eaten at a place acknowledged to be one of the top twenty or so in the nation. Not much of a contest, really. "Besides," I said to Peter, "we can always order Roquefort when they wheel the cheese trolley around."

Located on a peaceful avenue in a minimalist building that looked as though it might be home to a graphic design studio or a software company, Le Jardin des Sens means "the Garden of the Senses." It is both hotel and restaurant, the eating section a multi-levelled room in a spacious pavilion glassed on three sides. It has all the expected accoutrements: large tables with double white cloths, weighty cutlery and a bevy of faultlessly elegant waiters.

Picturing a room full of Chanel-clad women, I had agonized over what to wear. Black sweater and black pants will take you anywhere, I maintain, but I was mentally prepared for a slight elevation of waiterly eyebrows at the sight of Birkenstocks. It didn't happen, possibly because it never gets that formal in the

Languedoc, or maybe because the chefs, twin brothers André and Jacques Pourcel, and their business partner Olivier Château, who looks after the front of house and the wine, are all on the young side.

As befits its location between mountains and Mediterranean, the food at Le Jardin des Sens straddles land and sea. At least the lunchtime *table d'hôte*, the simple everyday menu, did: we weren't about to risk the multi-course midday feast that would, we suspected, leave us incapable of driving the three hours back to our cottage. Why we simply didn't give in and reserve a room for the night, I'll never know.

Prefaced by tiny delicious morsels to whet our appetites, the hors d'oeuvres arrived: gleaming silver sardine fillets lined up side by side on a cushion of herby potatoes; an airy terrine of rabbit and wild mushrooms. Then came our main dishes: a fat monkfish tail with a "lasagne" of fresh noodles, chard and eggplant; fanned slices of duck with a chestnut purée. Every mouthful was heaven. Across the room, the cheese trolley was reverently wheeled from table to table. Later, we thought, as we talked about our meal's ingredients: fish from the Mediterranean, vegetables from local growers, *cèpes* and chestnuts from neighbouring forests. It may have been sophisticated, but this was still authentic regional cuisine, inventive but not wilfully so, every ingredient tasting of itself. This was food that was *raffiné*, a French word that has so much more generosity, sensuality and a faint whiff of risk-taking than its pinched-lips translation (and you have to say this with a plummy English accent), "refined."

The brothers Pourcel preferred to edit rather than elaborate, we thought, until we got to the final course. First came the leisurely foothills of the *mignardises*, a plateful of jewel-like confections:

miniature pink meringues speckled with poppy seeds, cream-filled pastry tartlets cupping a single flawless raspberry, pastry boats with a cargo of some enchanting, apricot-flavoured substance, maybe ten varieties in all, and two of everything so that we could gorge guiltlessly. A brief pause and the waiter brought us vanilla mousse like clouds captured in a bowl, with the hidden surprise of fruit coulis at the bottom. Dessert itself was a grand finale, a great swaggering curl of caramel stretched across a wedge of rich but not overly sweet chestnut cake snugged up to a devilish chocolate mousse. With coffee came the final sweetener, a bowl of almonds, each with a thick carapace of sugar. To have tackled traffic right away would have been too abrupt a transition. Instead, we ambled into the Parc Edith Piaf just down the street and dozed contentedly in the late afternoon sun.

Only later did we remember that we had forgotten to ask for cheese.

Hmm, what's on "le menu" today? Almost every table d'hôte lists this salad. The unctuous, pungent cheese, the crispness of the "toasts" and the salad are a tasty combination. A small log of goat cheese is just the right size.

BISTRO SALAD

4 cups	mixed salad greens	1 L
8	½ (1-cm) slices of baguette, toasted	8
8	slices of goat cheese	8
	Vinaigrette (see below)	

Heat oven to 350° F (175° C).

Just before serving, place goat cheese on baguette and bake until cheese starts to soften and spread.

Meanwhile toss greens with vinaigrette and distribute on four plates. Top each plate with two of the baguette slices.

Serves 4

This recipe makes more than you need for the goat cheese salad. Refrigerate leftovers and bring to room temperature before using.

VINAIGRETTE

2 tbsp	wine vinegar	30 mL
	Salt and pepper to taste	
1 tbsp	Dijon mustard	15 mL
1/2 cup	good olive oil	125 mL

Place all ingredients in a small bottle and shake well.

CHAPTER 7

Anchovies and Art

COLLIOURE AND PORT-VENDRES

Going back to the source. For Peter, it's being there on the spot in front of the actual landscapes that an artist painted. For me, it's tracing an ingredient back to its origins, learning from someone who knows how confit is made or travelling to a village or town renowned for a single ingredient (although our proposed visit to Roquefort hadn't exactly been a major success). It's these background stories that enhance our respect and appreciation, for food or for art. With its promise of both, a day trip to Collioure was a foregone conclusion on our first trip to the region.

Anchovies mostly show up in Worcestershire sauce or Caesar salad dressing or as a contentious topping for pizza. We picture them tightly packed in a tin but forget that they are one of the most ancient ingredients known to Western cuisine; the first-century writer Apicius offers one recipe for cooking the little fish with oil, wine and herbs and another for frying them. Preserved, the fish's intense saltiness is a flavour as insolent and unequivocal as the taste of an olive. You can't be wishy-washy about anchovies: you either love them or you loathe them. I come down firmly on the side of the addicts. At the market in Mirepoix, the *bastide* town southwest of Carcassonne not far from our cottage, I frequently pick up a scoop or two of *anchoïade*, a creamy, intense purée that makes a pungent appetizer spread on toasted slices of yesterday's baguette, and I will often order a salade Niçoise just for its combination of hard-boiled egg and anchovy.

The fleshiest and most succulent anchovies anywhere are alleged to come from Collioure, and it would be gratifying to believe that the opportunity to track these small silvery fish to their birthplace, to come on a piscine pilgrimage, is what draws so many people to this hillside town on the coast just north of the Spanish border. But it's not true. It's the sheer gorgeousness of the place that attracts them. Ranged around a bay shaped like a clamshell, narrow streets of old houses clamber up towards the main highway that leads to Barcelona. Capped with a dome, the tall tower of the church of St. Vincent stands on a seawall guarding one side of the harbour. Close to its other side is the ponderous mass of the thirteenth-century Château Royal, once a Templar castle, then a palace annexed by, in turn, the kingdoms of Aragon, Majorca and finally France. Cradled between them is a beach where bright-coloured boats sometimes lie with their sails furled, a pleasant view for those of us who like to sit at an umbrella-shaded table in one of the waterfront cafés and order a *p'tit crème* or a *pression* or — a reminder that Spain is only minutes away — a sangria.

To painters, picturesque scenery and that pure clear southern light are a heaven-sent combination. Bristling with brushes, laden with palettes, eyes narrowed and pencils held at arm's length, they have been recording the luminous harbour of Collioure ever since Matisse popularized the site in 1905. Understandably, Peter was eager to do the same. While he hunkered down on the beach with his sketchbook, I set off to explore the Boulevard du Boramar, the promenade that runs parallel to the water, a place of seafood restaurants, postcard shops and little stands selling crêpes and ice cream that eventually leads to a small stony strand overlooking a violently frothing sea. Dramatic, primitive, it's a prospect that Matisse once painted using fearless strokes of indigo and aqua for the waves and red-brown and deep rose for the rocks. Displayed close by, a reproduction of the work reveals that the essential elements of the scene, the sea and the rocks, have not changed in the slightest. Collioure appealed to us strongly; as we drove away from it the first time we knew that we would be back one day.

Our initial attraction to the region was rapidly blossoming into a total obsession. A new year was now our signal to start dreaming about the next visit. When would we go? Possibly mid-May or June, staying till early July (Kate was now becoming accustomed to extended visits with friends or family), but never August, when every person in France climbs into their Citroën and goes on holiday with road-clogging results. September possibly, although that was a long while away. Then again, a visit of six or seven weeks starting in mid-September would let us experience the rich ripeness of a Languedoc autumn.

Drifting around Collioure one October morning while Peter decamped to the beach with his sketch pad, I could understand the powerful appeal it had for painters. Picasso, Matisse, Dufy and Derain were all mesmerized by the radiance of the town and the seascape. Its colour and vigour went straight to their fingertips; what they painted shocked cooler, more clinical minds in the north. It wasn't so much the brash use of reds and blues and ochres, it was the rapacious energy behind the brushstrokes, as if they were clawing at the canvas in their ferocity. Collectively they became known as *les Fauves*, the wild beasts, and their style of painting as Fauvism. In Collioure, you can follow a trail, *Le chemin du fauvisme*, that takes you to twenty sites (including the spot by the rocks) where Matisse and Derain set up their easels, so you can compare for yourself how little, or how much, the landscape has altered.

Rather than follow a designated route, I decided to wander with no destination in mind, mindlessly almost, just absorbing sights, sounds and aromas and seeing where they led me. In certain places, I thought as I poked around the back streets, in the Cathar castles for instance, your mind's eye needed to reconstruct the crumbling walls and to people the echoing stone chambers, in a layer-by-layer process of accretion akin to the art of the watercolourist. But in Collioure I wanted to subtract elements, to erase those souvenir shops, the estate agents' windows (this once-modest fishing village is now a highly prized — and priced — place to live), the densely parked cars, to restore the town to how it was when Matisse first saw it. Some aspects could stay.

I would keep the saffron gold of that façade over there, with its dark green painted iron balconies, and the visual abutment of those three houses at the corner, one pale pink, one glowing peach, the third warm white. I would also retain the *boulangeries* and *épiceries* and the dove-like French voices wishing each other *au revoir, bon appétit* as they parted for lunch, but I would lose the English one that noted jovially: "Bin a bit different, hasn't it?," just as I'd make all the pottery shops evaporate with their identical yellow dishes and bowls painted with olives or blobby blue flowers. The farther I got from the harbour, the more today's Collioure faded into yesterday's. Above the street women pegged laundry onto washing lines and watered geraniums, and ahead of me a man laden with grocery bags, the inevitable baguette tucked under his arm, unlocked his front door. Tail aloft, a silver cat stalked out. Life went on.

I wasn't nearly hungry enough to sit down to a proper lunch but I always have enough appetite to read menus in café windows. I love the pride that chefs in France take in using their local ingredients: mussels in Sète, *tellines* in Aigues-Mortes. In Collioure, unsurprisingly, it was *anchois* — anchovies. As *anchoïade* or in tapenade or in a *salade*, their pinky-brown fillets interleaved with strips of roasted red pepper or crisscrossing halved eggs, anchovies figure prominently in Collioure restaurants — as does another local product, Banyuls, a wine pressed from the grapes grown on the vertiginous terraced slopes that sweep down to the ocean. A *dégustation*, a tasting of this naturally sweet wine, was a temptation, but instead, as soon as Collioure reopened after its lunch break, I set off to bone up on anchovies.

On the drive into the town that morning we had passed two stores that sold them. They stood on the same street, one either side of the railway bridge, all that remains of what was once a thriving industry. Run by three generations of the same family since 1927, the Declaux establishment provided a solid introduction to the anchovy business through its collection of artifacts, photographs and memorabilia. Caught between May and October, I learned, the fish of Collioure are reputed to be leaner and tastier than their Atlantic counterparts. "They are distinguished by their dark brown colour," explained a sign on the wall, "and have firm and beautiful flesh and a rich and fruity flavour." The local reputation for anchovies dates back to the Middle Ages, when the port specialized in salting other fish too, such as tuna and sardines. Today, there are only three anchovy salters left in Collioure. Huge empty tins, old account books, a photo taken in 1930 of women mending nets while the fishermen looked on — this petite museum was a monument to an industry.

Next door, in the white-tiled shop, I met Sandrine Chastel. A pretty young woman with a nose stud and multiple ear piercings, she was a modern anchovy expert. She told me I could have my anchovies plain, like the ones she was cleaning with brisk, efficient fingers as she talked, but with my aperitif I could also try anchovies marinated with garlic or basil or shallots and capers or green peppers. Anchovies seasoned with curry spices were a local specialty, she added. Anchovies with lemon or — the traditional combination that's hard to beat for flavour and appearance —

red peppers were other possibilities, and then there was the onion and peppercorn variety ... I smiled and said honestly that I wished I could buy all of them.

Just down the street is the shop run by the Roque family, its two rooms filled with jars and bottles of anchovies. Here I could purchase *filets d'anchois à l'huile* in big 1000-gram jars, enough anchovies preserved in soya oil for a lifetime of Caesar salads, or anchovies preserved in salt in quantities up to 3300 grams — enough for several generations. Outside the door to the upstairs atelier, a sign regretted that "our friends the animals are not admitted." A handwritten addendum in bold black ink read: "Cats in particular." The scene in the anchovy factory within, blue-tiled and filled with ocean smells and cheerful talk, had probably not changed in decades.

Fresh anchovies can be macerated in vinegar to create *anchois blancs* or cured the traditional way in salt. How long they stay in the salt barrel depends on their size, the temperature and the season. Colour, odour, taste — and experience — tell the *saleur* when it's time for the next stage. Once the process is judged complete, some anchovies are rinsed and packed in oil and others are preserved in salt: I watched as an aproned woman positioned whole anchovies in a jar, coiling them so that they lined it. She packed the empty core with coarse salt, then added more fish, expertly twirling the jar in her hands as she filled it. Other workers filleted anchovies with

their fingers, stripping off one side and laying it onto a sheet of thin paper, then deftly whipping out the anchovy's backbone and placing the other fillet, slightly overlapping, beside it to form a tidy row.

Stocking up on these salty little fish or eating salade Niçoise down by the harbour, we invariably spend more hours in Collioure than we intend to. On every occasion we planned to drive farther south, but somehow it never happened until one year, late in October. This time our temporary home was a *gîte* (the term for the holiday homes that the French rent to one another) in a village called Léran. A handy five minutes from a road that led south to the Pyrenees and north towards Albi, it made an ideal base for excursions to Carcassonne, Castelnaudary and once to Andorra. ("Why go to Andorra?" Peter asked, rhetorically: "Because we can.") On this particular morning we intended to bypass the turnoff to Collioure, drive to Port-Vendres, a few kilometres to the south, and be home before dark, a day trip with a schedule that, in hindsight, was jinxed from the start. To miss market day in the local town of Mirepoix ten minutes away (in the wrong direction) was unthinkable; and then cheeses and produce had to be taken back to the gîte and unpacked. So it was one in the afternoon before we even glimpsed the Mediterranean from the highway, beyond the red-tiled roofs of Collioure.

I suppose we could have had a quick snack when we arrived in Port-Vendres, a *croque monsieur* or a sandwich inside a café, but the day was glittering, effervescent; admittedly there was a flinty wind in the shadows but it felt unseasonably warm for October by the harbour's outdoor restaurants. "The proprietor also owns fishing boats" reads the business card of the Café Pujol. We learned that later, long after its *table d'hôte* menu had hooked us into settling in at a table. Three courses for not many francs. Even before we got into the first of them, a waiter set down an *amuse-gueule*, a palate-teaser, of mussels and aïoli, the golden garlicky "butter" of southern France.

Peter's fish soup arrived with the traditional accoutrements of rust-red *rouille*, shredded cheese and "toasts," but as always tasted subtly different from others he had eaten. (It never ceases to amaze us the number of variations that French chefs can play on the classics. Then again, how many ways are there to play Beethoven or Hamlet?) My plate of chilled *coquillages*, both cooked and raw, was a picture-perfect collage of oysters, clams, whelks and a *petit* red crab, a mattress of damp green seaweed protecting them all from their bed of crushed ice. Next? The main courses arrived: a hefty paella, salt cod with a creamy garlic sauce, and vegetables, among them a tiny croquette made, as far as I could judge, with as much cream as vegetables. Midway through we ordered another half-litre *pichet* of white wine. Then came an apple tart and a piece of chocolate cake with crème anglaise, feathered with chocolate sauce, and by the time we had sipped the last of our coffee and spent a recuperative half-hour stopping in at the tourist office and climbing up and down the narrow pink-tiled flights of steps (called *rampes* not *rues*), it was getting rather late.

And we hadn't even followed our intended plan of a walk to the end of the harbour.

Badly damaged during World War II, Port-Vendres doesn't pretend to be soaked in history, but it's an attractive little

community whose houses and shutters seem to be tinted to laugh at the pitiless Mediterranean light: white with turquoise; pink with dark wine red; pearl grey with a jaunty marine blue; even the church is a cheery pink with a blue-green dome. But all of these paled beside the extraordinary riot of colours in a giant stack of fishing nets down by the harbour. We stopped a few feet away and gazed. My first thought was: what a sweater this tangle would make. There were flaming scarlets, oranges, salmon pink, palest rose and every shade and tone in between in the red spectrum, from barely pink to a colour as deep as cassis. The colours went on: aqua, a golden-green, a watery grey, a turquoise as dark as the sea and a turquoise the colour of verdigris, pale caramel, wistful lilacs, the bronzes, russets and dull greens of pheasant feathers, all looped, swagged and draped into one explosive assemblage of colour, lighter on top where the sun and salt air had faded it, richer, even more vibrant inside. At one end, a rusty chain, copper coloured and flecked with blue-green, looked carved from semi-precious stone; floats, faded to the soft reds of Edwardian book jackets, edged the net like a necklace of trading beads.

A fishing boat docked and we watched as its metallic catch was unloaded, then immediately put up for sale, to be eaten that very night. By now, the sun was dropping down the sky with the speed of a child descending a playground slide, the light quickly dimming. Ahead of us lay a winding drive through a gorge in darkness.

"Probably behind an enormous truck," said Peter. "Why don't we stay overnight?"

"I don't have my toothbrush."

"So?"

It took minutes to find an inexpensive room in the Hôtel du Commerce which overlooked the harbour.

Eight p.m. That night in Port-Vendres, halyards jingled as the waves gently juggled boats from hand to hand. Street lighting and the few neon signs sent down shimmering ladders of gold, green and magenta into the water. Lunch was just a memory. Maybe the fish we had seen earlier would be on the menu for dinner. But tourist season had ended and most restaurants appeared to close as we approached them, lights clicked off, chairs were placed upside-down on tables, until the only option left was a mobile pizzeria. We ordered the simplest, topped with cheese and tomato, and consumed it on a bench facing the harbour.

One reason for coming to this particular place was, as in Collioure, to see the reality of what had been interpreted in art. But where the town just up the coast made a major production about its connection with Dufy, Matisse et al., you could walk around Port-Vendres all day and see no evidence of someone equally well-known — probably because skill with pigment and canvas was the least celebrated of his talents. His tea rooms, his design for an art school in his native Glasgow, his spindly ladderback chairs, even his unique leggy lettering had all become instantly recognizable even to non-artists or architects, but Scottish icon Charles Rennie Mackintosh had another side too: he was also a painter.

He recorded cathedrals and cloisters in his travels to Europe, he drew sinuous women in the art nouveau style and botanical sketches in pencil and watercolour. He held a number of exhibitions. But by the early 1920s his star had waned and in 1923, depressed by repeated rejection of his architecture and design, Mackintosh and his wife retreated to the more affordable life offered by southern France, settling in various little communities including Port-Vendres. He designed no houses here, no idiosyncratic furniture or stained glass windows. What he did, to the exclusion of all else, was paint. For the last four years of his life, till illness forced him home to Britain to die, he created images of the landscape around him, rendered with painstaking but unrealistic precision. Where Dufy and Derain some twenty years earlier had depicted the southern French landscape and architecture with dashing sensuality, Mackintosh reined in his emotions. He may have absorbed the curved stones, wonky shutters and irregular surfaces of a typical southern French house façade, but he reinterpreted it all in architectural terms, every line as precise as if marked with a ruler, every angle a right angle: nature reduced to a flat pattern. Mackintosh was a slow, meticulous painter who only worked outdoors when the weather was fine. Even though he spent several years doing nothing but painting, his output was small. Of his time in France, we had read, only thirty-eight works survive, all landscapes, almost half of the Port-Vendres area and just two of Collioure; the coastal path between the two villages was a favourite evening stroll for him and his wife.

Beside the harbour in Port-Vendres that night, we indulged in a little conjecture. Surely, we hypothesized, given the length of time he was here, Mackintosh must have left *something* behind. Asking around earlier that day had proved fruitless. Staff at the local tourism office and at an art gallery said that, as far as anyone knew, Mackintosh had taken all his work back with him to Britain where it eventually ended up in galleries and private collections. But what if he hadn't?

The possibility continued to nag at us the following morning, especially when we learned that Mackintosh had stayed in that very hotel. The day was grey as we walked along the quay, a voile curtain of cloud masking the blue sky behind it. Outside the Café Pujol, a young man scrubbed down the outside of the seafood tank. In a waterfront bar, a man in a beret sipped coffee as he calmly read the soccer results. WALL STREET IN FREE FALL read the front page headline. The Mackintosh trail had grown cold. If there were no dusty *brocantes* to sift through in hopes of unearthing a forgotten sketch, where else was there to look?

"I think we should try Collioure," said Peter. "You know that hotel ...?" It was on our route home anyway.

We drove north along the coast, headed into the town past the anchovy packers, parked the car on a side street and made our way down towards the beach to the Hôtel des Templiers where, for umpteen years, painters have traditionally paid their bills in art. One time, in the bar over a coffee, I had counted almost a hundred works, hung two and three high up to where they touched the dark beams. Not an iota of wall space was left vacant. Murky landscapes, anatomically suspect nudes, spurious "Fauvist" interiors with off-kilter perspective, it was all here. If, we reckoned, Mackintosh had left anything behind from his sojourn in France, this was the place to find it.

The bulk of the collection hangs in the hotel's corridors and stairwells but, "oui," we could certainly look at them, said a member of the hotel staff. So we climbed the first flight of winding tiled stairs and started searching, leaning over the bags of dirty laundry that lined the corridors, the timed lights going off periodically and leaving us in darkness. Studies of bulbous-cheeked babies needed only a swift glance, as did paintings of cows. Among the many images of Collioure was a signed Dufy (*a signed Dufy?*) — sailboats, dark scribbles of waves, a sky full of breeze.

Then, just outside room number thirty-three, *voilà!* We immediately knew the small painting in front of us came from the hand of Charles Rennie Mackintosh. The identifying signs were all there: the muddled patchwork of fields organized as a flat plane; the rigorously geometric buildings with windows indicated by small precise brushstrokes; the northern palette of muted greens and browns. It was unsigned and undated (as was much of his work) but it was unquestionably a Mackintosh. Of course, we had no proof that it was an original, but why would someone copy a painting, then choose to hang it in such an obscure location as the corridor of a small French hotel?

Still, what was needed was concrete proof and, back in North America, that took some time to find. Most reference material on Mackintosh focuses more on his architecture, interiors and furniture than on his paintings. Eventually we tracked down an out-of-print book whose author, Roger Billcliffe, listed every watercolour he had been able to locate in eight years of searching. We found it immediately, more or less identical in composition and colour to the one we had discovered — even the configuration and position of a cloud was the same. The painting in the book was more "finished" too. "That one in the hotel was probably a sketch," said Peter, a rehearsal for the finished work. A nice theory but, in fact, we learned a couple of years later that the "sketch" had been painted very skillfully as a prop for a film on Mackintosh. The authentic version is now in a private collection. The "faux" one is still there, close by the harbour that inspired an entire art movement, and not far from the anchovy boats.

Stay long enough in the Languedoc and you start viewing anchovies as a staple. This simple first course is adapted from a recipe I picked up in Collioure at the Roque family store.

ANCHOVIES À LA CATALANE

2	large red bell peppers	2
1	tin anchovy fillets, in oil, drained	1
4	hard-cooked eggs	4
1/4 cup	chopped parsley	60 mL
3	cloves garlic, finely chopped	3
1/4 cup	vinaigrette (see page 135)	60 mL

Roast the peppers under the broiler until blackened and blistered on all sides. Place in a bowl and cover with plastic wrap. When cooled, skin and seed peppers, pat dry and cut into thin strips. Arrange prettily on a platter with the anchovy fillets and hard-cooked eggs. Sprinkle parsley and garlic over all and drizzle with vinaigrette. Serve with chunks of country bread.

Serves 4

CHAPTER 8

Paella and Snails

PERPIGNAN AND
CATHAR CASTLES

Saturday morning in Vancouver. Friends are coming to dinner tonight. I'm making paella from a recipe in Julia Child's The French Chef Cookbook, a paperback so battered that its front and back covers have both fallen off. I go to the local public market and wander around the stalls, thinking wistfully of the "halles" of Narbonne and Béziers. Nevertheless, I'm able to buy the chorizo, the clams, the mussels, the shrimp — I'm trying to be as authentic as possible. I've yet to taste paella in its native Spain, and later that afternoon as I follow the first steps in the lengthy recipe I begin to wonder how far this North American translation has evolved from the original Spanish. One chilly autumn evening in France, we find out.

J ourneying to the region over and over again, we were slowly
enlarging our social circle, maintaining the links from afar
through Christmas cards, letters and increasingly by e-mail.
There were more and more people whose dining tables we had
sat around, whose kitchens we had stood and sipped Blanquette
or Fitou in, but while we had often enjoyed their hospitality,
we were not always able to return the invitation. We got our chance
one summer when our English friend Ben, who lives permanently
in France, visited Canada with his close *amis*, Isabelle and Didier.
Sipping wine out on our deck as the day faded and the Thai
chicken grilled on the barbecue, talk turned inevitably to
differences and similarities of cooking, to the fast-food culture
prevalent here and now infecting France and then, circling closer,
to local variations of Languedoc cuisine. Knowing that Isabelle
was Spanish, I asked her about paella.

"There is rabbit," she said, "and a fish — I don't know the
name in English. Next time you're in France, come to *our* house
and I'll make you a real Spanish paella." We would be over in
three months' time but probably wouldn't have had the nerve to
take her up on the invitation if she hadn't insisted on writing her
and Didier's phone number on a scrap of paper and finding a
space on our fridge door for it among the photos and postcards.

"There," she said. "So you won't forget."

We didn't. Late one October afternoon we set out from the
remote stone-walled cottage in the Pyrenean foothills that was
our temporary home and drove west through a long, forest-lined
valley. The light was greying by the time we spotted Didier in
his blue car, waiting as arranged at the side of the highway just
beyond the town of Foix. He was right: without him to lead the
way, we probably would have got lost. The side road he took

unspooled across farmland, looped through villages and made abrupt right-angle turns before it ended at the farm where the couple lived. We parked in the open barn amid a typically bois-terous rural greeting of clucking and barking. By then darkness had descended but the house brimmed with light, warmth and the kind of smells that make your stomach gurgle. Other guests rapped on the door: a curly-haired museum curator and his ram-bunctious black dog, a neighbouring woodworker, his wife Odette and their two rangy teenage sons. While the men sipped wine, Odette and I adjourned to the kitchen, not only to keep Isabelle company, but also to watch her make a real, *auténtico* Spanish paella.

In fact, all we'd be seeing were the final stages. She had already done much of the work, she told us, and now it was mostly a matter of assembly. Brought from her native Spain, the paella pan was close to a metre wide and stood on an equally large waist-high gas burner. Isabelle poured in olive oil and, when it shimmered with heat, added rice. As it spat and sizzled, she ladled in steaming broth, blending it in with a flat wood stirrer. "What's in the other pots?" I asked, pointing to a phalanx of saucepans on the stove. Handing the stirring over to Odette, Isabelle lifted the various lids to show me. There was rabbit and chicken (both from nearby farms) and fish (the small shark caught in Mediterranean waters). Onions, tomatoes, garlic and juice from the mussels cooked ear-lier would go in too, she said. "This is paella, Valencia style," she continued, "my mother's recipe." Her family traditionally put in chickpeas as well, which may not be authentic, she added (inter-estingly enough, so does Julia Child).

Stir, stir, add ingredients, wait for all the savoury flavours to get friendly with each other … Fifteen minutes later, you could have bottled the smells that filled the kitchen, aromas so tangible they were almost visible. The rice had absorbed the rich stock, meats and fish had been set on top and now it was time for the garnishes. While Odette arranged plump pink shrimp around the rim, Isabelle organized strips of roasted red pepper and I filled what spaces were left with mussels. She called in Didier to help her bear it triumphantly into the dining room and we all sat down.

"In Spain, paella is often divided into wedges," Isabelle told us as she portioned it out, "and where we have plates, there it might be eaten directly from the pan, in which case woe betide anyone who lets their fork wander outside their serving," she said with mock severity. We didn't, but we did devour almost the entire panful, not to mention the dessert that Odette had brought (two cakes so good I asked for the recipes) before climbing into our car and following Didier back through the black night to the main road.

Serving paella in a French household sounds like an anomaly but it's not. Eating Spanish food in the western part of the Languedoc, now known as the Roussillon, isn't at all unusual, and it's logical when you look back in time to the centuries following the Roman occupation. Like a shuttlecock in a royal game of badminton, a large chunk of today's Roussillon region was tossed back and forth between the kings of Spain and France before finally passing into French hands in 1659. By then, the cuisines of both countries had vigorously intermingled.

Food is as influenced by history as it is by *terroir*, that glorious mixture of geography and climate. These days, jet travel plays an increasing role. Living in Vancouver with its enormous Asian population, we are as likely to eat fresh Shanghai noodles as linguine for supper and when we hear the word "dumplings" we think of little shrimp-filled *har gow* before the kind that float in soup.

On our first visit to the Languedoc we couldn't find balsamic vinegar on supermarket shelves, but by now it was everywhere and ready-to-heat *nems* — French for egg rolls — sat next to the croques monsieurs at the takeout counter. But while globalization was definitely entering the picture, locals were still using local ingredients, as they had done for centuries.

Culinary archaeology of a sort was what drove me when, the following June, after a week on business elsewhere, I flew to Toulouse and caught a train south to Perpignan, the most Spanish town in the Languedoc, about twenty-five kilometres north of Collioure. I was off in search of *cargolade* — *cargolada* in Catalan, a language similar to Occitan.

The *cargolade* is not so much a dish as a social occasion, a time for feasting when friends get together outside to grill snails over a fire of vine clippings and eat them with bread and aïoli. This unique regional happening is traditionally held on Easter Monday or Whitsunday, though in practice a family reunion or gathering any time of the year is a good enough excuse. Centred on food and bonhomie, it's a carnival event: everyone pitches in to prepare and cook the snails, and the sausages and pork chops that usually accompany them. A salad follows, and later there are peaches or grapes or Catalan desserts.

Throughout the feast, wine washes down throats made dry by fresh air, woodsmoke and lively conversation.

The chances of happening upon a real *cargolade* were as remote as the hills they often take place in, especially as I was on my own this time and getting around by rail made going off the beaten track a difficult proposition. Then again, cassoulet and confit were now staples of urban life: maybe I would get lucky here, I thought as the train pulled into Perpignan station, the same station that Salvador Dali maintained — incomprehensibly, I felt when I saw it — was "the centre of the world." I left its bland surroundings, carefully positioned my backpack and set off, like a human snail, to walk the seven blocks to the Hôtel l'Avenir. My room was charming, with walls and furniture hand-painted with grapevines and scarlet poppies and a window looking out on a terrace and the Perpignan roofscape. Compared to the simmering heat outside, it was also wonderfully cool, so comfortable that I was vaguely tempted to buy a chilled beer from the friendly Madame at reception, exist on the bread, cheese and fruit I had with me, and read till sunset. But I couldn't resist going out right away on the trail of the snail.

Fate, a look at the restaurant listings in Les Pages Jaunes in the hotel's lounge, and a not too judicious guess at its cuisine, took me to L'Assiette Catalane ten minutes away. The menu outside did indeed list *cargolade* and inside, gaily striped table linen, rough-cast plaster walls and Picasso posters reflected the French-Spanish fare. I ordered a carafe of rosé, "*et cargolade, s'il vous plaît.*" Not tonight, the waiter replied, our snail supplier is closed on Mondays. Bad news tempered by good news. What snail supplier? I noted his name and made do with tapas: a plate laden with anchovies, tomato wedges, a single *couteau*, roasted peppers, chewy country ham, chunks of chorizo, a pale orange crescent of Charentais melon and *pa amb tomàquet*, a popular Catalonian snack made by rubbing bread with tomato.

Words like *pa amb tomàquet* are not just on menus. The Latin-based language of Catalan is everywhere in this vivacious, flower-filled city, including its bilingual street signs. Rue de la Barre — Carrer de la Barra — had, I read the next morning, bustled at various times with meat, vegetable and fowl markets. Its name, which it was given in 1585, referred to the bar that once spanned the street and from which game, chickens, fish and other edibles were hung. Not far away, in the Place de la République, cheerily painted sculptures of mermaids and sailors adorned the outside of the indoor market. Clustered near the entrance were stalls blazing with apricot-coloured chanterelles. I registered them but only vaguely, intent on my destination at the end of the square: the modest shop of Raoul Nepy, the snail merchant.

I was back at the source again. On a stall outside, hundreds and hundreds of snails, shells striped grey and sand yellow, reposed in rectangular plastic baskets, green plastic trays over-head keeping the inhabitants moist and content. Snails are like shrimp, I observed; price is directly connected to girth. *Les grosses*, the big fat ones, were for *la cargolade*. I was interested? *Attendez.* Monsieur Nepy's employee sped into the dim depths of the store and emerged with an odd-looking utensil, a small-holed metal funnel with a long curving iron handle. He slid the lid off a snail basket, picked out an especially large specimen and showed me how to use the device — called a *capucin* — to drip melted fat into the snail's shell as it grilled.

Here were all the elements for a *cargolade*: wire grills, round, square, small and large; strings of taut-skinned red onions; bunches of herbs and bundles of vine clippings. I asked Monsieur Nepy's employee where the snails originated, but he would only say they were found locally, no more than that. He was sure, however, that the place just down the street served them, and, *voilà!*, steered me two doors away to a revolving rack outside a *tabac*. It may be hard to find in reality but a *cargolade* is a popular image for postcards.

With the well-meaning snail enthusiast hovering right next to me, I felt obligated to buy one. I also took his advice about restaurants and, accompanied by the metallic rumbling of shops being shuttered for lunch, made my way along an alley to the quiet courtyard that is home to The Troubadour. I scanned the menu. No *cargolade, malheureusement*, but soon a brown pottery dish was sitting in front of me filled with snails prepared Catalan-style, small snails far too little to get a firm grasp on with the tongs; after a few ineffectual tries, I gave up and used my fingers. Each was a long semicircle of meat, pale at its foot, darker at its tip. Often it took a sharp tug to wrest the snail out of its home and it curled up on itself as it exited, splashing juice on my shirt in a post-mortem act of revenge. I tipped the emptied shells over the dish so that any remaining juices could add to a sauce that was red, fiery and already intensely flavoured with diced ham, tomatoes and peppers. As I scooped up the last of it with the largest snail shell, I thought what an ideal dish *escargots Catalane* was for a midday meal in France. It was tasty, it was the original slow food, and it was non-fattening. Like the *tellines* I had eaten in Aigues-Mortes, the energy expended on eating snails probably consumed more calories than they contained.

There was still an entire afternoon to while away, and all of Perpignan to explore, before I could return to L'Assiette Catalane for the hoped-for *cargolade*. I idled back to the Place de la

République, past the shuttered snail store and through a maze of back streets to a small square and the Cathedral of St. Jean, whose unassuming exterior didn't begin to suggest the magnificence within. The gumdrop colours of stained glass were all I could see at first in the meagre light but then, as my eyes adjusted, I noticed the red marble floor and the soaring nave. Its height and airiness seemed supernatural, as if the builders of this cathedral had received divine but practical aid from a fleet of sinewy angels who, flying high above a sheet of stone as malleable as fabric, had used their celestial crooks to pull the lofty vaults into being.

Outside, sticking to the narrow ribbon of shadow at the side of the street, I made my way to the massive hexagonal walls around the palace that was home at various times to the royalty of Majorca and Aragon. The latter kept lions in the castle ditches; meadows inside the bastion were reserved for the sheep that made up their daily diet. The palace was closed for some function or other, but I had better sightseeing luck down by the river at the Castelet, a sombre red-brick building once a prison, now a folk museum whose exhibits supplied lively proof that kitchens and métiers may change but food remains much the same. A mannequin of a shepherd was attired in a red cap, corduroy pants and white linen shirt and carried a water bottle made from a *calebasse,* a long-necked gourd. Ferociously spiked collars protected his dogs from marauding wolves. These men cared for their stomachs as well as their animals. Elsewhere in the museum, a painting showed a shepherd preparing his *cargolade* supper, a net bag bulging with snails on the table, his *capucin,* flagon of oil and a cloth-wrapped loaf at one side. In the background stood a woman, his wife presumably, with a tray holding something round, brown and undoubtedly edible.

That evening, worried that the chef might run out of snails before I got there, I was back at L'Assiette Catalane early to order *cargolade* — the Catalan shepherd's supper, the small intimation of what this grand celebration must be. My plate arrived and on it a little wire grill with a central handle, similar to those I had seen at Monsieur Nepy's. On top were snails, juices still bubbling, shells slightly charred. There was bread and a pot of pale yellow aïoli. I wanted to make a small ceremony of this. I took a slice of baguette, spread it lavishly with aïoli and inhaled its garlicky fumes. The snail I speared was sizzling hot and larger than the ones I had eaten at lunch. I gently placed it on its aïoli-blanketed bed and took a sip of chilled rosé to prepare my palate. Then I bit in. The crustiness of the bread, the rowdy marriage of garlic and oil, the meatiness and almost gamy taste of the snail, the contrast of heat and cool: it was a felicitous combination and I made the pleasure last, sucking each shell clean of its salty, smoky residue before moving on the next.

The following day, June 21, marked the official start of summer, the day when communities all over France celebrate with music. In Perpignan, what seemed like every schoolchild from miles around marched through the streets blowing instruments and banging drums. Cars waited patiently; everyone was in a festive mood — and every restaurant in town offered a special menu. "A lunch to be reckoned with!!" I wrote in my journal of the first course, a salad involving confit of *gésiers* (duck gizzards), *lardons* (morsels of bacon) and foie gras, which I ate at an outdoor café whose paper tablemats showed the place as it had been a century earlier. Not much had changed. I ploughed on through poached cod with aïoli and scoops of lemon and blackcurrant ice cream. Meanwhile a moving braid of humanity shifted back and forth in front of me: young girls with milk-chocolate tans and skirts no larger than cushion covers; couples entwined like bindweed; boisterous packs of teenage boys, and old people getting their daily airing. A dachshund tethered to a café chair towed it into the pedestrian traffic all to the mingled music of Catalan folk tunes (just up the street) and modern French pop (at the corner), one more symbol of Perpignan's place as a crossroads between France and Spain.

It is also the site of the pivotal traffic circle where you can leave the coast with its pale beaches and turn inland towards the land of the Cathars, as Peter and I did later that year. Soon the flat green vine-striped plain starts to crease and bulge. Speckled with scrubby bushes, mole-brown hills rise on either side, the prone legs of a giant whose lap is a vast vineyard, empty except for the occasional hut, like a miniature cottage, where those who tend the vines keep their tools. For much of the year this is a still, calm, sleeping landscape where the sun beams down and the grapes fatten and grow juicy. But by late September the valley is dotted with pickers — like oversized insects grazing among the leaves, big plastic buckets strapped to their backs — and tractors towing open trucks laden with glistening purple caviar for the great god Bacchus. Positioned like sentinels along this strategic valley, proud and seemingly unconquerable, are Cathar castles built on its uppermost pinnacles.

The road begins to follow the course of the Maury river and, in the village of the same name, we turned right and aimed for the peaks to the north. Our destination was not nearby Peyrepertuse, a small walled city like a miniature Carcassonne with ramparts ninety-two metres long, but the mightiest castle of them all, Quéribus, which stands guard over the entire plain of Roussillon. Looming through the fog and rain that often descend on these hills, its silhouette is like a stone staircase climbing into the clouds, so exposed to the elements that climbing it on a windy day is a treacherous undertaking. Even on this jewel-bright autumn afternoon, with the air still and the sun a diamond in a blue enamel sky, Quéribus had a feeling of foreboding about it, its ruins like gargantuan rotten molars socketed into the jawbone of the rock. Attempting to capture it must have been a daunting task those long centuries ago. Even after you take the long route up from the valley and climb the monumental crag that is its foundation, the castle still towers high above.

Here, in the Corbières wine region, is the heart of what is now called "Cathar country." Postcards and maps and signposts show you how to follow the trail of sieges and carnage from one site to another, going, for example, from the four castles of Lastours on their rocky peaks and Minerve on its limestone promontory, both on the rim of the Black Mountains north of Carcassonne, to the three-towered town of Foix in the west to the ruins embedded in the hills of the Pyrenees. Quéribus was not the first Cathar castle whose heights we had scaled but it was unquestionably the most dramatic.

Within the massive stone walls at the summit, the wind buffeted and roared as we explored rooms that were shadowy even at noon on a blazing day. How its inhabitants must have welcomed each dawn, and how they must have dreaded the months when winter came raging down the valley, a great angry exhalation, chill and spiteful, like death's own breath. The wind bellied out our T-shirts as we ascended into a lofty chamber where winding stone steps took us to the top of the *donjon*, the great tower that is the highest point for miles around, the highest point in the world it seemed, a vantage point over the entire region; from here you could surely touch heaven. We looked down at peaks far below us, across the Roussillon plain to a road no wider than a fingernail scratch, then down at the vertiginous drop to the ground below. How could anyone possibly conquer *this*? Yet Quéribus, the last Cathar stronghold, fell easily to the Catholics in 1255, eleven years after the symbol of Cathar strength, Montségur to the west, had capitulated after a long siege. It was the beginning of the end: the movement gradually died out and, in 1321, the last believer was burnt at the stake.

From the base of the castle, a wide trail wound downhill into the countryside. Leaving Peter behind to set up his easel, I started walking. It was October but the earth was still parched, offering evidence of the hammer blows of the midsummer sun. Vegetation had to be tough to survive here and it was: a grey-green landscape of thorny juniper, sturdy thyme and everywhere — now that I could spot the subtle differences in colour and shape that defined individual varieties — lavender bushes, their flowers grey and hollow this late in the season but still intensely perfumed. When I pulled at a stalk, the plant was so desiccated it rattled. I had always wondered why lavender, a flower, was often included in the classic mixture of *herbes de Provence* and now it made sense: they share the same soil.

As we deepen our knowledge of the sites connected to the Cathar story, we've come to recognize that each has its own distinct personality. Quéribus feels like a place of utmost power and authority; Montségur, where the tale reached its sad conclusion, is, not surprisingly, drenched in melancholy. But not every castle echoes with the sounds of clashing steel. Farther along the road that leads inland and west from Perpignan is the château of Puivert, its square tower visible from miles around, its atmosphere more one of culture and merriment. It is said to have been a gathering place for troubadours, whose songs of love in the melodious Occitan language delighted medieval courts. The troubadours were gallants who, some maintain, created the notion of romantic love. In an era when marriage was based more on uniting property than bringing together two mutually passionate people, this was a novel concept. That said, their desire, expressed through poetry and song, was usually focused on a married lady, a woman of the court and invariably chaste.

Like the troubadours and the women they wooed, Puivert was dedicated to pleasure rather than warfare and played a minor role in the Cathar story. In 1210, at the beginning of the Albigensian crusade, Simon de Montfort seized it after a siege lasting a mere three days. Its peaceful history means it is still well preserved. Passing through the gatehouse, we entered a grassy courtyard framed by a rampart punctuated by six towers. In the centre stood a square keep, four storeys high: four vaulted rooms, one on top of another. As we climbed the narrow, spiral staircase, window slits framed faraway fields, precise squares of brown and umber, like a checkerboard. In one room, known as the minstrel's hall, eight lamp brackets, each carved with a musician and his instrument, anchored the ribs of stone that straddle the ceiling like a spider's legs.

It took little imagination to picture flickering candles casting shadows on the stone floor or highlighting the polished wood of a cithara or rebec. While these are instruments long vanished from the vocabulary of music, others have evolved into forms we know today, like the vielle, which became the violin, and the *tambourin*, an early drum. In the village of Puivert, a small museum displays working replicas of these instruments re-created using fourteenth-century stone carvings as reference.

Commercialization of these sites is, understandably, in direct proportion to their accessibility. Both Quéribus and Puivert charged admission and sold postcards; Roquefixade, which stands to the east of the Ariège town of Lavelanet, did neither. Erosion has carved enormous gullies down the rock that is its foundation, and the site, originally known as *roca fisada*, the cleft rock, predates the castle, which was built in the eleventh century and torn down by order of Louis XIII in the 1600s. Crusaders never attacked Roquefixade, although it is said that the villagers lit beacons on its peak to communicate with the castle of Montségur, visible across the lushly wooded valley.

On an achingly beautiful autumn morning, the village of Roquefixade seemed the most benevolent of places, and the ruins that tower over it appeared an undemanding ascent if the wide cart-track that led from the main square was any indication. Along the verges, ferns had dried blonde, chestnut and bronze, like a hair-colouring advertisement. The hillside across the valley was draped with a thick chenille shawl, a uniform dark green except where random flashes of copper or lime marked the changing of the leaves, the main road that carved through it so far away that traffic sounded like sighing surf.

Leaving Peter to set up his easel in the village's deserted square, I followed the remains of a road, abandoning it when it continued on towards a nearby hamlet and branching off on a small trail that angled steeply up towards the rear of the castle. It was shady there and suddenly chilly, a place of thorny bushes; my heart bumped like a jackhammer at the gradient. The path ended abruptly and I realized that the only possible route to the castle was via a cramped, shrub-lined fissure in the rock. I squeezed my way through, emerged on a grassy plateau and saw the village far below me, the square with its fountain, the tiny figure of Peter at his easel. Standing on the edge of the dizzying drop, I waved vigorously. Crickets chirped and an invisible pack of hunting dogs barked its way across the forest opposite, a distant gunshot suggesting they were on the trail of a wild boar. Beyond these hills rose the pewter-coloured, snow-topped peaks of the Pyrenees.

The sound of the church bell drifted up from the village and, immediately afterwards, a discordant tangle of smaller bells sounded as a flock of sheep streamed out from a barn. At this distance the animals were no bigger than cells seen through a microscope, swarming across the village square and vanishing down a side street.

Even though I knew the descent would be laughably easy, a matter of skipping and sliding down the hill, I didn't want to leave Roquefixade. There were no signs to point out this or that, no arrows to direct me, no brochures, no postcards, no people: I had the place to myself — and my reveries. I faded the scene to grey in my mind and then, as it grew dark, watched villagers who had taken refuge here, their cloaks wound around them against the cold, set light to a beacon, sending its beams across the valley and waiting for the tiny responsive pinpoint of fire from the other side. Back to the present day, I ambled around its green spaces, releasing the scent of wild thyme with every footstep. Birds cast gliding shadows and a tiny gecko made the grass shiver as it whisked by. Otherwise all was still. What an ideal spot for a picnic. The remains of fires showed others had thought so too. I could imagine the crackle of flames, the crunch of bread, the smell of garlic. Probably hundreds of people, villagers, neighbours, had met up here over the centuries. And then it occurred to me — what a God-given place to hold a *cargolade*.

As Isabelle told us, everyone has their own version of paella. Use this recipe as a jumping-off point, and experiment with different varieties of meat and fish. Add peas, green beans or, like Isabelle's family, chickpeas.

If you don't like mussels, leave them out and include more shrimp. Once you have the technique down, you'll find this a simple dish to prepare even on a weeknight. Leftovers, if any, reheat well.

PAELLA

12	fresh mussels or clams	12
12	large shrimp	12
2 tbsp	olive oil	30 mL
2	fresh chorizo or hot Italian sausages, cut in 1/2-inch (1.5-cm) slices	2
1 lb	pork butt cut into 1/2-inch (1.5-cm) cubes	500 g
4	chicken thighs or drumsticks	4
1	large onion, sliced	1
3	cloves garlic, finely chopped	3
2	tomatoes, coarsely chopped	2
4 cups	stock (made with the mussel juices plus additional chicken stock)	2 L
	Large pinch saffron	
1	bay leaf	1
1/2 tsp	paprika	2.5 mL
	Salt and pepper to taste	
2 cups	rice	500 mL
2	red bell peppers, roasted, skinned, seeded and cut into thin strips	2
1	lemon, cut into wedges	1

Cover the bottom of a large saucepan with water. Add the mussels, cover and cook over medium-high heat until all the shellfish open. Drain the mussels, saving the cooking liquid, and refrigerate both.

Bring a large pot of water to the boil. Drop in the shrimp and cook until just pink (about two minutes). Drain and refrigerate.

In a large frying pan, heat olive oil over medium-high and brown the sausage. Pour off excess fat and add the pork cubes and chicken. Sauté until golden. Set aside. Reduce heat, add the onion and garlic and cook until softened.

Measure reserved mussel juices and add chicken stock to bring total up to 4 cups (2 L).

Return the meats to the pan, add the tomatoes, stock and seasonings. Cover and simmer over medium-low heat until the chicken is almost cooked, about 20 minutes.

Bring the pan to the boil and stir in the rice. Return to the boil, reduce heat to low, cover pan and let cook for 15 minutes. Remove the lid and arrange mussels, shrimp and red pepper slices like spokes of a wheel. Continue cooking for 5 minutes or until rice is cooked and garnishes are heated through.

Garnish with lemon wedges and bring to the table.

Serves 4

CARGOLADE

Re-creating an authentic cargolade outside France is impossible unless you can get hold of live snails, which is unlikely. You can, however, get a garlicky breath of its flavour by serving canned snails, heated and drained, with slices of country bread, toasted or not, and a big pot of golden aïoli.

AÏOLI

10	cloves garlic	10
1/2 tsp	salt	2.5 mL
1	large egg yolk	1
1 cup	olive oil	250 mL
1 tbsp	lemon juice	15 mL

Whizz the garlic and salt together in a food processor until minced. Transfer the mixture to a large bowl. Whisk in the egg yolk until thoroughly blended.

Trickle in the olive oil very, very slowly in the finest possible stream, whisking as you go, until the mixture thickens. Whisk in the lemon juice.

Use immediately, or keep refrigerated for up to three days.

Makes about 1 1/4 cups (300 mL)

CHAPTER 9

Arugula, Nuts and Fungi

RENNES-LE-CHÂTEAU
AND MONTSÉGUR

I'm looking at strawberries. In February? Why would I even consider them when I know that, sliced in half, their insides will have no more colour than Styrofoam — and about as much juice and flavour. France has spoiled me. It's also altered my grocery-buying habits. And our predominantly rural lifestyle has, in some odd way, fused Peter's enthusiasm for colour with my obsession with food. Now I have come to see the calendar as a paint-box. The winter months are the pale tones of confit, cabbage and potatoes; May and June are green with asparagus and wild dandelion leaves; July and August are pages soaked in the warm gold of peaches and nectarines; the harvest months are the russets and browns of walnuts and mushrooms.

I nspired by what I was learning from French friends, I had become an ardent forager. Why refuse what nature set out with such lavish generosity? By now, I knew specific places where we would find certain fruits and vegetables, and the most likely time they would appear. Not that time of year seemed to matter with one particular crop. Whether it was spring, early summer or autumn, I knew we could always rely on two things in the hilltop village of Rennes-le-Château, twenty kilometres east of Puivert. The wind would whistle and howl as we walked around its streets and, on a more practical note, I was sure that we would always drive away with a hefty bunch of wild arugula on the back seat of the car.

This arugula is not the miniature salad green served in smart restaurants or even the forthright sort, known in France as *roquette*, that I have spied on occasion in the indoor market at Lavalenet. It's a vigorous rogue variety, its robust frilled leaves dark green, its flavour a lively dispute on the palate between mustard and walnuts. For several years my source in Rennes-le-Château was more than a plant; it could only be described as a *bush*, growing behind the broken-down wall near the spot where we usually parked. I had never seen such a prodigious amount of arugula in one place. Then, one year, it disappeared, but scouting around in search of the distinctive leaves I discovered another prolific, if smaller, source flourishing at the base of a tower, a tower that seemed oddly refined for a location this rural, jutting out from the hillside to provide a God-like view of the long valley.

Oddities and God are closely connected in Rennes-le-Château, a community that thousands believe is the repository of a secret so cataclysmic that it could rip accepted Christianity asunder. The story that lures visitors has all the elements of a mystery novel. In 1885, fresh from the seminary, a new *curé* arrived in the village. His name was Bérenger Saunière. A photograph of the time shows a comely, dark-haired man with a generous mouth and strongly marked eyebrows. It was a humble posting, this pastoral care of a community not far from where he was born and raised, and, as all the ensuing literature stresses (and there are enough books and pamphlets to stock a small library), Saunière received the usual meagre stipend due to a village priest.

A sanctuary since the sixth century, the church is dedicated to Marie de Magdala — Mary Magdalene — the same Mary said to have fled to the south of France following the crucifixion, and whose church we had seen in Stes. Maries de la Mer. Consecrated in 1059, Rennes-le-Château's church was dilapidated and in dire need of repairs by the time Saunière became the priest there. But his income was too sparse to stretch to restoration; for that he had to tap village funds. He started his renovations in 1891, and the mystery begins. Part of his work involved removing the altar stone which rested on two ancient columns. Closer examination revealed that one of these was hollow and concealed four parchments that had safely slept through the centuries in a sealed wooden container. Rumour has it that some of these parchments displayed family trees, while others showed curious quotations. Either way, and as an honest priest should, Saunière took the documents to his superior, the bishop of Carcassonne, who instructed him to bring them higher up the ecclesiastical ladder to Paris. Three weeks later he returned to Rennes-le-Château and the story might have ended there, forgotten, if Saunière had not behaved so bizarrely in the years that followed.

He spent like a drunken sailor, coiling a new road from the base of the mountain up to the village, erecting a crenellated

tower — the Tour Magdala, at whose base I had found the salad greens — and a library that looked far down the valley and was connected, via a terrace that curved along the lip of the mountain, to a winter garden. He built a comfortable bourgeois house, the Villa Bethania. He collected fine textiles, china and books, spending the equivalent in today's terms of millions of francs, an amount that far exceeded his priestly income. The village gossiped. It was all very strange. Saunière even died peculiarly, of a sudden stroke in 1917. Not suspicious perhaps, except that some days earlier, while he was still in robust health, his housekeeper had ordered a coffin for him and, summoned to hear his deathbed confession, a fellow priest refused to administer the last rites. Saunière left behind obvious questions. What was the source of his immense and unexplained prosperity? Did he discover a treasure hidden by the Knights Templar — maybe even the Holy Grail itself? Or had he perhaps unearthed information in the parchments that would shake the roots of Christianity itself and been "paid off" by the papacy to conceal it? And why did he build such a very curious church?

You expect Paris to be romantic and Nice to be glamorous. Travellers overlay their own preconceptions on any place, even one they're seeing for the first time, and Peter and I are no different. Your own mood also plays a significant role in your initial impressions. It's possible that, unaware of the Saunière mystery and beneath a blue sky, we might have viewed Rennes-le-Château very differently. But it wasn't just that: an incident en route had left us both feeling sombre. As we stopped to investigate a small village, an elderly woman approached us and our routine *bonjour* opened floodgates. As we walked along, she spoke of her dying village and her dead husband, of winter, of loneliness, of watching the same TV programs over and over, of the school that had closed and the church that only holds services once a month.

She left us at the gates to the cemetery and we drove on, numbed by her sadness. It had also made us nervous about choosing a location to live in. Could we rely on instinct to steer us away from a place that, maybe not now but five years down the road, would feel as dead as this village? We talked about it in the car, and about a widow so lonely she would tell her troubles to strangers. Had we been in a less pensive frame of mind we might have seen Rennes-le-Château as just another village. But I don't think so, and to be fair, a sign at the turnoff from the main road does invite you to "Discover the mysterious world of Abbé Saunière." What exactly would we see? The four kilometres up to the village was ample time for speculation.

From the windy hilltop the landscape seemed designed for a deity to play with. How easy it would be from this vantage point to rearrange the small houses in the town of Couiza far below, or to crack the thread-like roads like whips and shake the rumpled land like a tablecloth to smooth out its rugged escarpments. Deserted houses and crumbling walls gave the village a defeated, desolate air and the wind blew with real savagery as we made our way towards the church whose roof, framework and vault were all paid for by Saunière out of his purportedly minuscule wages. A rooster crowed. Ivy strangled a stone tower. Over a side gate was a carved stone skull.

From the outside the church is square, solid, grey and unexceptional except for the Latin inscription above the entrance:

terribilis est locus iste, usually translated as "this place is terrible." Just inside the door is a font, nothing uncommon about that except that, crouched beneath it, eyes glaring, mouth a square cave of rage, is a carved black devil, one hand splayed like a claw. Odd, very odd. And it could have just been his deplorable taste or a rural parish priest's attempts at grandeur, but the church's interior seemed more decadent than holy, its walls tinted boudoir shades of peach, lemon yellow and violet blue. Miniature gargoyles protruded from the gilded canopy over the pulpit and coin-like silver circles dotted the ceiling. The glass eyes, unnervingly real, of the religious statues appeared to follow our progress. The sickly colours, garish designs and enigmatic Stations of the Cross have been interpreted in numerous ways; even the shadows that fall through the windows on certain days of the year are said to have special significance.

I had never seen a church like it, or such an ominously quiet village. There were no men playing *boules*, no *boulangerie*, the one café was closed and the liveliest place around was a bookshop whose sign bore a crudely painted devil and promised more than 666 titles. Inside, formless new-age music wafted over the sound system and you could buy crystals, tarot cards, astrology books and shelves full of endless theories about the mysteries of Rennes-le-Château.

The village hit the headlines in the 1970s through a series of British TV documentaries and *The Holy Blood and the Holy Grail*, a book that blended hard facts, intensive research and speculation that Saunière had, indeed, discovered an astounding secret: the Son of God had not died on the cross but had been smuggled alive across the Mediterranean to southern France, where he had wed Mary Magdalene and founded a dynasty. That theory is only one of many: Internet sites detail the ever-growing web of hypotheses. Some visitors maintain that the immediate area holds the key to the secret of the lost continent of Atlantis. I've heard that one local is so convinced that UFOs will land on her property on Judgement Day to scoop up the righteous that she has built a landing strip for her alien rescuers. Esoteric movements are centred here. A book I glanced through claimed that if you draw lines connecting the principal local landmarks, you create a pentagram. Is Rennes-le-Château Christ's burial place? Does it conceal a message for mankind? Is it a doorway into other dimensions?

We retreated to an information centre where Louise Robin, a middle-aged English woman in tweeds, was sorting pamphlets. "The 'treasure' is unknown," she told me; "I'm open to any suggestion." But there is proof, she says, that Saunière sold holy masses. As for the ominous inscription over the church door, in her view, "It depends how you translate it. Terrible can mean awful — or awesome." Nevertheless, armed with clues, interpretations and hunches, twenty thousand people a year descend on Rennes-le-Château. Some dig for treasure: "We spend all winter filling in holes," Robin said dryly. One man, she told me, flew in from Hong Kong just to verify a personal theory. People in the village hate the story, she added, which perhaps explained the cold looks and the woman who scuttled past us, face concealed by a black scarf.

Of all the theories, one that appealed to us strongly was the notion of Rennes-le-Château as the door to another dimension on the Day of Judgement. We even tried to find the apocryphal UFO landing strip. As we drove around searching, the wind whistled spookily in the telephone wires and swept across the green grass, feathering it with waves of light and shade. The gravel road we had been told to take wound on and on but nothing came into sight, least of all a runway, and as twilight deepened we turned back. This is not a place I would care to get lost in at night.

While some believe that the Holy Grail itself is buried at Rennes-le-Château, others maintain, and have done since the thirteenth century, that it was concealed at the fort of Montségur, which fell to the Catholics in 1244. About forty kilometres from Rennes-le-Château, south of the town of Lavelanet, the ruined castle looms on the horizon, its bleak walls rising to the summit of a steep-sided 1207-metre pinnacle in the Pyrenean foothills. From the road that curves partway around its base, Montségur appears indomitable, impossibly high. It was inconceivable that an army could capture an edifice that boasted such an advantageous position. The first time we saw it up close we sat in the car picnicking on a baguette, cheese and pâté, watching swags of cloud like layers of muslin being pulled aside by the wind, alternately hiding and revealing details of the castle's stark structure, its mighty leviathan of a rock dotted with dark tufts of trees. It looked indomitable but we had heard it was surprisingly easy to climb and the well-trodden walk proved to be fairly undemanding, initially zigzagging up through brush and bushes, eventually becoming a steep, stony track that led to the base of the walls. Below us, the sun threw a spotlight on Lavelanet. An army of hills receded into the distance, the blue-grey of the farthest dissolving into the blue-grey of the sky.

Within the castle walls, all was silent except for the faint sighing of the wind. All that remains of the interior are the stone outlines of rooms and, halfway up the exterior walls, the square holes that show where wooden beams once rested. Back outside, we noted just two arched entrances and several precipitous drops. It seemed impossible both that hundreds of faithful had lived in and around the fortress and that they had not been able to withstand a siege till the end of time. In fact, it took less than a year for the castle to fall.

Even with nothing left but the walls, the silence up here made us question how life must have been for the fugitives. How did they tolerate the winters, which are frigid at this elevation? Inevitably, I also wondered about how and where they got their food. Did they forage among the trees below? Did they have adequate supplies of grain on hand? And on non-food matters, what resistance would they have had when massive rocks fired from catapults crashed in their midst? Did their faith keep them going amid what they must have realized was a hopeless situation?

In the spring of 1243 the crusading army had arrived at Montségur. Occupied since prehistoric times, its very name — "safe mountain" — indicating an impregnable haven, Montségur was the head of the Cathar dragon: it had to be lopped off with hailstorms of arrows and the bone-crushing attacks of enormous catapults. The village museum contains evocative evidence of the assaults the castle suffered and hints at the life the besieged Cathars must have lived within its walls. What they left behind was pitifully little — a few links of chain mail, some blackened and roughly forged harness buckles, a few arrowheads — but the very smallness of these objects emphasized how frail their protection was against the might of the crusaders. Scale models also brought home the power of the various throwing machines that may have been used to attack the castle. One, which required more than a hundred men to operate it, could hurl stone balls weighing 100 kilograms — the size of a rugger player — as far as 220 metres. On display is one of the balls that landed in the castle, over a foot across; others were reused for paving the courtyard. In a display of muscular Christianity, the Bishop of Albi doubled as cleric and engineer during the siege; it was he who prepared the trebuchet, the mighty catapult, for use.

The attack raged all that summer and on through the snows and rain of winter, and it wasn't until the following year that the besieged of Montségur capitulated. The mountain was suddenly silent. More than two hundred Cathars filed down to a spot at its foot, where they were clustered together and burned at the stake. Close to the Prats del Cramats, the "field of the burned," a path angles down towards the village of Montségur, the start of a route taken by the survivors who fled to Spain. Now called Le Chemin des Bonshommes, it extends 193 kilometres to the Spanish town of Berga. One day, we tell ourselves, one day.

Montségur dominated our daily lives on several of our stays, its ponderous shape our backdrop for almost two months, its magnificence and the hills surrounding it framed by the tall window of the cottage we were staying in. We had borrowed the cottage from Nigel, our English friend who has lived in the Languedoc since the mid-1990s and is gradually renovating a row of formerly tumbledown dwellings. Each place we stayed in was playing its part in crystallizing our vision of the kind of house we wanted for ourselves. Living here on a remote hillside confirmed for us that we didn't want to be on a lively street — although we did want to be in a lively village (but not on its main road, a key question we had now learned to ask before we drove miles to view a *maison de village*).

In this place with its view of Montségur there was nothing but peace. Every day opened and closed with the tinny clang of cowbells and, quite often, we had to wait for sheep to move as we tried to drive along the rutted cart-track that ended at the house. The cottage is so isolated that it's a tiny dot in a field of green on the aerial-view postcards we send with "X — this is where we're staying" written in the margin. Remote doesn't begin to describe

a place that is a fifteen-minute drive and seven hairpin bends from the nearest town. To start with, the road rambles across a bucolic landscape, past fields of cows and sheep and farmhouses, before coming to a crossroads where it narrows and begins its ascent into the hills, the forest of oak, beech and chestnut trees falling away abruptly at the side of the road. Walking from the cottage to the town takes almost two hours, downhill all the way. I cannot begin to guess how long it would take to make the journey back.

Across the valley, Montségur looms in my vision as I roam the hillside next to the cottage, its pasture clipped as close as a croquet lawn by the cattle, sheep and goats that graze here. Not far away, just past the gate in the fence, is a stately chestnut tree and, some distance beyond that, shortly before I reach the stand of trees that conceals a ruined farmhouse, are juniper bushes, vicious thorns protecting their blue-purple berries (dent a ripe one with your thumbnail and you realize where gin gets its flavour). In the other direction, a forty-five minute walk towards town, stands a walnut tree, scrawny but prolific. We may be far from civilization but, as at Rennes-le-Château, it is fine countryside for foraging.

The arugula I harvested at Rennes-le-Château always ended up in the salad bowl or layered with cheese and tomatoes on a length of baguette. The blackberries I picked on the hillside needed only a dollop of crème fraîche, the extra-thick variety. I shelled the chestnuts I gathered, cooked them till tender, mashed them through a sieve and sweetened and lightened the purée with sugar and crème fraîche. While both were worth hunting for, the best autumn crops of all were the wild mushrooms. Cleaned, sliced and tumbled in hot butter, they made a lusty side dish with grilled chicken or fish, or contributed fleshy texture and musky depths to a ragout of beef.

Also flavouring our last few weeks here was a definite poignancy. It was years now since we'd first decided to buy a home in the Languedoc but we still had not found *the* place. Between visits, we would continue the hunt, combing websites and waiting for the monthly issue of *French Property News* to arrive in the mailbox.

"There's an English bookshop for sale with a two-bedroom flat over it ..."

"But that probably means no garden. In any case, do we really want to be tied down to a business?"

While other people we heard of seemed to buy French houses on a whim, the right place continued to elude us. By the time the millennium rolled around, all that we had acquired was a new understanding of the nuances of real-estate language. We knew that *beaucoup de commerces* meant shops in the village and, if you were lucky, a café and post office. *Un hameau* was a hamlet with no permanent *commerces* at all: you must be ready when the travelling *boucher* and *boulanger* pulled his truck into the square and tootled his horn. A *ruine* was just that, a ruin. We dithered between buying somewhere in a village and somewhere so isolated that we would be nervous about leaving it empty for months at a time.

As anywhere else, words could be duplicitous — they just sounded more appealing in French. We learned to ignore the siren call of any advertisement promising an *ancien* house with *beaucoup de cachet* and *vaste* rooms: all it meant was a colossal dump with medieval plumbing and an annual heating bill that would make the national debt look like small change. *Habitable* indicated you could live there, technically speaking, if you didn't mind washing in cold water and using a toilet in the barn. A *calme* village, or rather *hameau*, meant the bread truck's daily visit was the high point of excitement for the community's five inhabitants.

This particular visit had almost come to an end. The days were shortening, the temperature dropping, and a hearty casserole was always welcome. In late autumn, the view from the cottage window changed daily as the leaves became a fabric of gold, orange, red and brown. As the nights grew colder the stitches of this leafy tapestry weakened and fell away, exposing the pale warp and weft of trunk and branch. Making our way up the road after dark, we could now see the lights of the town through the trees, like stars trapped in a dark net. Day by day, the landscape was turning from a painting in oils to an etching.

Amid all this death and decay, plump, earthy and moist mushrooms seemed like nature's last gasp of growth and fertility. Out on the hillside, with the sun at the right angle, I could spot the white gleam of field mushrooms from a hundred feet away.

I was familiar with these from growing up in England, but not the tall hooded pale ones that rose like periscopes from the field or the small globes that exploded in a puff of spores if I inadvertently kicked them. More than two hundred varieties of fungus have been found in the region and, around here, mushroom-hunting is a popular occupation, especially at weekends when the sides of the track towards town are peppered with Citroëns and Renaults. Late in the day, we frequently see the hunters emerging from the woods bearing lumpily bulging bags.

In autumn, I always wear clothes with capacious pockets in case I stumble on some walnuts or chestnuts, but mushrooms need more delicate treatment. A mushroom likes a basket or a brown paper bag; in a plastic bag, it quickly turns slimy. I knew that, but I had nothing else with me the morning I came upon an especially fine crop of fungi. After lunch, my morning's haul carefully placed on the backseat, we drove towards Mirepoix through the umbers and ochres of the year's grand finale. Baked by the heat, sunflowers had dried to a brownish-black, heads drooping, standing in rows like an army of penitents. Corn still stood in the fields too, the cobs left to harden for use as winter fodder, husks as crisp and pale brown as ancient papyrus.

The pharmacy on the main square in Mirepoix was in an autumnal mood as well. Instead of the usual lotions, creams and unguents, its late-October window saluted the hunt. I've never understood the mixed message of the toy rabbit dressed in camouflage with a gun tucked under his arm (or seen this particular character anywhere else), but the models and posters of fungi alongside him are there for good reason: to help amateur mycologists identify, and eat, only those varieties that are safe. More help is within. In France, it's part of a pharmacist's training, and a job requirement, to be able to identify mushrooms. Bag in hand, I went inside and joined other customers waiting on the bench. It seemed odd to be there, surrounded by bottles of nail varnish, constipation remedies and herbal teas, clutching my mushrooms. The old woman next to me peered at my lap. "*Un sac plastique? Non, non, non …*" she said emphatically before I could protest that I didn't usually … had never before … normally wouldn't dream of using plastic. Her politesse overcame her. I was a foreigner in dire need of help. She swiftly put names to what was good —

"*Lépiote ... champignon des prés*" — and what I must discard, a lone puffball: "*un vesse-de-loup.*" The pharmacist echoed her right down to the stern admonition not to use plastic and gave me a poster that did more than identify fifty-one varieties; it also provided recipes and — just in case — listed the phone numbers of poison control centres.

"I'M SITTING ON a rock on a hillside looking right across at the great hump that is Montségur," I wrote in my journal later that week. "It doesn't get much better than this." And it didn't. There was almost no sound except for a breeze stirring the dry leaves on the trees, the occasional drone of a fly and the small scratching sound as a leaf joined others on the ground. The mountains opposite surged up like colossal dark breakers, wave upon wave, with the hill of Montségur like a magnificent cresting sea beast. Before me, striped with animal tracks, the pasture sloped down like the seats of an amphitheatre. Once this hillside was terraced and farmed intensively, Nigel had told us, and there were people living here by the early Middle Ages. As late as the 1950s, five families lived in the hamlet, their only sources of water the rain and a spring three hundred metres down the mountain. Most of them were shepherds and farmers, with one exception. According to local lore, he made his living as a mushroom picker. I wondered if he too occasionally looked across at Montségur and speculated about the brave and hardy Cathars who had lived there eight centuries ago.

Imagine a taste midway between mustard and walnuts. That's arugula. Adding both to a salad really brings out this green's wonderful flavour.

ARUGULA AND WALNUT SALAD

| 4 cups | arugula | 1 L |
| 1/2 cup | walnut pieces | 125 mL |

DRESSING

2 tbsp	wine vinegar	30 mL
	Salt and pepper	
1 tbsp	Dijon mustard	15 mL
6 tbsp	good olive oil	90 mL
2 tbsp	walnut oil	30 mL

Wash and dry greens, wrap in a clean teatowel and refrigerate until needed. Place in large bowl and sprinkle walnut pieces over.

Shake dressing ingredients together in a small bottle. Toss salad with just enough dressing to lightly coat the greens. Store leftovers in the fridge for tomorrow.

Serves 4

Look for chanterelles or cèpes at farmers' markets. While you can eat this dish from bowls with toast on the side, far better to my mind is to sit the mushrooms on the toast so that all the fungal juices drip into the bread — a treat to save for last. Feel free to add more butter or garlic.

WILD MUSHROOMS ON TOAST

1 lb	wild mushrooms	500 g
3 tbsp	butter	45 mL
1	clove garlic, finely chopped	1
1 tbsp	chopped parsley	15 mL
	Slices of rustic bread, toasted	

Clean mushrooms and slice thickly. In a large frying pan, melt the butter and add the garlic. Cook gently for a few minutes until garlic starts to soften. Add mushrooms, cover pan and cook until mushrooms are tender. Sprinkle with chopped parsley. Serve on, or with, toast.

Serves 4

CHAPTER 10

Sparkling Wine and Ripe Apples

LIMOUX AND MIREPOIX

Let's go there in May or even June, I say. From my January vantage point, I can almost count this in weeks. Even though these are fine months to be in Vancouver, I want to be in France on midsummer's eve, on the longest day of the year. Besides, if Kate, now eleven, comes with us, she won't miss as much school. Also, I add, if we're there in June, we can eat ourselves silly on peaches.

The end of a radiant June day, our skins still warm and salty from an afternoon by the sea. We are sitting in the stone courtyard of a village house we have rented with a view to buying. We are tempted by its romantic tower, with a bedroom at the top where we can look out over the ridged roofscape, but dissuaded by its quirky central courtyard, which means that even to take a platter of fruit from kitchen to living room we have to step outside. We intend to spend half the year in France eventually, and must keep in mind that this would be frosty in November, although it is more than fine in flaming June.

On our way to the beach that morning, we had picked out a dozen superb peaches in the Béziers market, their downy skins the colour of blushing amber, their flesh so opulently ripe that we knew if we didn't consume them within hours they would be squashy and brown the next day. Some we devoured at the beach, rinsing our sticky fingers in the waves, but there were still a few left. Their voluptuousness, and the simmering evening, suggested Bellinis, whose mix of peach juice and champagne is the essence of sun and celebration. But the house we were living in, owned by North Americans, though well-stocked with designer sheets, lacked the basic equipment found in any French kitchen. Specifically, I discovered after a thankless root through the drawers, there was no gadget to purée the peaches, no strainers, no sieves, no conical Mouli. Peeling the fruit was easy, I did it with my fingernails, the skin sliding off like a silk robe, but how to extract the juice? I tried mashing chunks of peach through the tiny wire mesh basket of a tea infuser, a tedious and messy process. The second peach came in for rougher treatment, but it worked. I simply squeezed the skinned fruit in my fist, wringing it like a sponge into a tall glass jug, the excess juice running down my forearm and dripping off my elbow onto the flagstones.

Renting different places over the years opened our eyes to the varying emphases that different countries place on food. Show me a kitchen and I'll tell you the nationality of the person who owns it. "Holiday homes" that belonged to people who spent most of their time in North America seemed to assume that you would exist on take-out food. Whatever their nationality, home-owners who lived in France year-round took it for granted that, even on holiday, their renters would occasionally roast their own chickens or make their own soup. And French-owned *gîtes* were invariably the best equipped, complete with a Mouli in the kitchen cupboard. In fact, it was a must, as I discovered later from a *gîte*-owning English couple who were full-time residents. They showed me the equipment list supplied by the French govern-ment, which would have done credit to a professional kitchen. Saucepans of various sizes, frying pans ditto (although cast iron ones were forbidden), chopping boards and good knives, a deep-fat fryer, an electric mixer, an assortment of cake and *tarte* tins: all were on the inventory "advisory." Also required was a sardine key but, oddly, no kettle or teapot. All of which suggested that the French cooked with as much enthusiasm *en vacances* as they did at home. And that *maman* rarely sat down for a quiet cuppa.

Let's hope she spoiled herself, as we were about to do, with an aperitif. Peter cracked open the chilled Blanquette de Limoux, releasing a satisfying "thup" sound followed by pale smoke like grape bloom from the neck of the bottle. The wine hissed like seafoam as it hit the peach juice. Effervescent and just a little sweet and fruity, Bellinis are, to my way of thinking, the finest possible drink for a sultry summer night.

The authentic version gets its kick from champagne, the bubbly invented by Dom Perignon in the late seventeenth century. I wonder if he was aware that, far to the south, some other ecclesiastics had already beaten him to it? Ever since the 1530s, the monks at the Abbey of St. Hilaire had been fermenting locally grown grapes in bottles, and the region around the town of Limoux, south and slightly west of Carcassonne, has long been famous for its sparkling Blanquette, a word that means "white" in Occitan.

Blanquette besides, the *bastide* town of Limoux with its grid of streets and an arcade-framed market square has a lot to recommend it. But its appeal is more than just architectural or vinous. Every Sunday from January to March is a carnival day when costumed and masked revellers perform traditional dances to the sound of brass bands, a tradition dating back to medieval times. So, I suspect, do some of the recipes served at La Maison de Blanquette, where a flute of the local fizz is the customary start to your lunch or dinner. Set back from a busy road across from a *boules* court, the restaurant is unimposing and used to be a love-project of the wives of the local wine growers, eight or nine of whom volunteered in rotation to handle the cooking and serving. Vigorous ladies with a passion for gourmandise, they would pour you Blanquette almost before you had a chance to sit down at your table and were not averse to having a glass of their husbands' vintage behind the bar themselves.

The mostly local clientele spanned all ages. Any evening you might see intense young lovers, stately grandparents, groups of young men in sweaters and jeans and parties of four in business suits, all carefully perusing the menus. One night we watched as three generations entered the restaurant together and the winemakers' wives clucked and cooed over the newest, a babe, before leading everyone to a corner table where *le petit* could sleep quietly, his basket cushioned on the banquette, and *maman* could turn away unobtrusively to provide her son's evening meal.

In this homey setting, at tables spread with pink cloths and white lace, we nibbled braided wreaths of anise-scented dough with our Blanquette. The menu of profoundly traditional Languedoc cuisine sometimes offered a salad of goat's cheese on garlic-smeared baguette, slid under the grill and served on frilly green frisée dressed with a light vinaigrette so deftly made that we polished our plates to mop up the last of it. On other occasions we have devoured confit of duck gizzards, ruby-dark and thinly sliced, accompanied by thyme-scented slivers of home-jellied ham. Limoux is particularly famed for its fricassee, another of those rural dishes so suited to the chill winter climate. The version here is made from nuggets of kidney, slices of liver, thin discs of *cornichons* and chunks of pork shoulder, cooked so slowly and lovingly and long that they're practically falling apart, and served with a separate steaming bowl of pale brown beans. Exhaling garlic, the pottery bowl of cassoulet meant to feed one would, like all cassoulets, have satisfied two. On the cheese tray stood Cantal, a goat cheese sagging with ripeness, a white jug of fromage blanc and a jar of honey, the piquant tang and smoky sweetness a felicitous mixture on the tongue.

As we coasted towards the end of dinner, stuffed as local ducks, one of the Mesdames would come along and lead us through the list of desserts: *tarte tatin* or crème caramel or *crème catalane*, a limpid creamy custard flavoured with fennel seeds that's a specialty of the region; and then, saying this with a smile of inner delight at the thought of it, "there is ice cream: *nougat* or *chocolat* or *marc de Blanquette."* We couldn't decide. "How about *un mélange?*" An evening spent at La Maison de Blanquette was like being adopted into a tribe of genial aunts. To prolong the experience, we usually purchased a bottle or two of Blanquette before waddling off into the night through the echoing streets and driving cautiously back to Chalabre or Léran or wherever else we were staying through the banks of fog that drifted like furtive grey cats across the road.

That's how it used to be, until sometime in the mid-1990s when the restaurant changed hands. The fare still has the same sturdy authenticity: the fricassee of Limoux, the chicken cooked over a wood fire and the cassoulet are still on the menu. But last time we were there the wine growers' wives had been replaced by whippet-slim young men and the photos of the winemakers at ceremonial dinners were gone, their place taken by stuffed heads of *sangliers* (wild boar) and deer. Indeed, the room in general owed more to taxidermy than interior decoration: a fox and various birds lined up on the mantel and a stuffed black bear standing on a rock held centre stage on a table. All reminders that this was hunting season, when everything from large fearsome boars to small birds was under siege.

To an eagle riding the air currents, the road from Limoux to the town of Mirepoix must resemble an unravelled ball of grey yarn. Not the direct route that the trucks thunder along, but the longer way via Chalabre, a winding and far prettier journey. As the car winds its way forward, the layers of rotund tree-covered hills ahead appear to slide back and forth like cardboard cut-out scenery in a children's theatre. The umber walls and tawny roofs of farmhouses lurch across a ridge or rest, far below, in the V of a valley as though they had grown up through the earth,

the vine-striped slopes gradually giving way to meadows and pasture as the land flattens out.

While Limoux is synonymous with Blanquette and, to a lesser extent, its fricassee, to a classically trained chef in France or anywhere else in the Western world, the term *mirepoix* indicates one of the building blocks of authentic French cuisine. The man who gave his title to this mixture of finely diced onions, carrots, celery, ham (sometimes) and herbs all gently sautéed in butter, and whose chef invented it in the first half of the eighteenth century, was the splendidly named Charles-Pierre-Gaston-François-de-Lévis, Duke of Mirepoix. As the aromatic foundation for all manner of ragouts, soups and sauces, his *mirepoix* has spread far and wide but, until recently, the town that carries his family name was less well-known.

If there is a more appealing *bastide* town than Mirepoix, we have yet to find it. My heart jumped on that first visit back in 1993 when we walked through the stone gateway called the Porte d'Aval, all that remains of the original ramparts, and found ourselves in a handsome square that has barely changed in five hundred years. We had been catapulted back to medieval times. Around us were tall, half-timbered houses, three storeys high, their dark wooden beams prominent against façades and shutters painted raspberry, buttery ochres, greens, honey and lilac, the colours luminous in the late afternoon sun. Jutting out some four metres, the upper floors create generous arcades that shade and shelter café tables, the newspaper and postcard stands outside the *presse*, and clusters of people in conversation. The beams that support the houses and span the arcades are the hue of dark chocolate and time has weathered them to iron-like hardness. Outside the establishment known as the "house of the consuls," now a hotel, some long-ago craftsmen carved faces and animals at the ends of the beams (some are erotic, we have heard, although careful examination has failed to find anything remotely titillating).

"Okay if I just sit here and draw?" said Peter, unfolding a portable stool.

"Half an hour do you? No, let's say a quarter to four in the café." We've played this scene out more times than I can remember.

Making sketches or scribbling notes on our own or meandering together, we have spent countless indolent hours in and around Mirepoix's main square and maze of streets, never failing to discover some new pleasure: a glimpse through a doorway of a sunlit garden; a shop window filled with antique toys;

a store that sells good wine, local sausage *and* implements for performing minor veterinary surgery all under the same roof. But those are afternoon pursuits; our morning routine is more structured. Bag of sticky, buttery *pains aux raisins* in hand, we head for the end of the square and the Café Castignolles, the walls and ceiling of which are a uniform umber that, nurtured by the smoke of countless Gitanes, grows darker every year. Hung here and there are large yellowed photos of Montségur and Mirepoix and at the rear of the room, a roguish poster of a boy chasing a girl across a meadow, *culottes* at half-mast, his intentions abundantly clear.

Usually it's easy to find an empty table at the Café Castignolles, except on a Monday — and on Mondays it's mandatory to spend some time at the café because that's when

everyone you know in the region meets up at the market. Narbonne and Béziers may be home to our favourite *halles* — indoor markets — but Mirepoix is the indisputable champion of the open-air variety. By eight in the morning there are stalls everywhere, filling the square and set up near the cathedral under the covered market with its impressive iron canopy. It's as if a great pool of people and everything they require to make daily living worthwhile has been dropped into the marketplace, from where they have flowed out into the surrounding streets. Farmers selling livestock cluster around the base of the fourteenth-century cathedral: chickens rustling in cages, bright-eyed and knowing roosters, geese, ducks, a serene brown rabbit or two in a cardboard box. Sitting at a small table that holds a few bunches of thyme, bundles of carrots and a handful of beans, an old woman counts out speckled eggs so large that every one must surely be a double-yolker. Stout-bellied men in blue pants and caps catch up on the week's gossip, rooted like rocks, always in the same place, the crowds amiably swirling around them.

I take two things to Mirepoix market: an empty wicker basket and an open mind. Over here a stall is piled high with the new crop of garlic, its skins pinky-purple, its stalks bunched like bouquets. Over there the winemakers have lined up their bottles, jewel-like in the sun, with casks in the back of the truck ready to fill the *bidons*, the three- and five-litre plastic jugs used for *vin ordinaire*. The colours of the French flag come to life in scarlet geraniums, azure overalls and the bales of white lace used to make curtains. A cheese stall's creamy mounds and yellow blocks are identified by the valley, *col* (mountain pass) or region they come from. The beret-wearing cheese seller sings songs from the Basque country while his wife pares off samples and deals them out like playing cards to potential customers. Theirs is one of several stalls decorated with miniature models of cows, sheep or goats spelling out a cheese's provenance.

Standing over it all is the cathedral. The gargoyles stare down at us, crouched on the edges of the buttresses, their four paws together as though about to leap. Far from being terrifying, these are whimsical creatures that seem to have crept out of some French fable. Before they were cleaned up, one sported a neck-ruff of faded grass, another wore a cap of brilliant saffron lichen and a third was forever peeking around the clump of greenery that shared his perch. Inside the cathedral, the floor is of uneven flagstones and light gleams across the tops of the pews, polished by generations of hands raising bodies from devout knees. It's an immense soaring space with the widest nave in France, lit by *rondelles* of stained glass, its dimensions more concert hall than church.

Outside, the stallholders rarely change their places, so you know that if the man who sells chinaware is at the market today, he will be close to the cathedral door with his straw-lined packing crates holding white cups nested in rows: demi-tasses and larger cups for *café crème*. Bowls in three sizes are printed with tumbling blue grapes and sprays of cherries and strawberries. White china asparagus platters come with their own drainage rack. Cheese plates are painted with chunks of various *fromages*. There are little jugs meant for cream and gigantic soup tureens. A white dish shaped like a flat-bodied duck is intended for foie gras and designed, somewhat cruelly, so that the bird's turned head looks quizzically down at her own liver.

Sometimes, you can buy fresh foie gras at the market and, at a charcuterie stall, sausages rolled in pepper or *herbes de Provence*,

their stalky, leafy overcoat so dense that you would hardly guess there was meat inside. Other sausages are studded with chunks of walnut or hazelnuts; a slice reveals the hollow-centred filberts with their concentric rings of colour, like sections of meteorites. Shielding the edibles from the sun are square umbrellas, striped red and yellow or blue and white or the red-brown of the local earth. Some are scallop-edged like the waves that wash the sand near Sète; others crenellated like Carcassonne's battlements. At times like these, the food, the history, the buildings seem magically interconnected. Into the basket goes a jar of honey like golden fog and a squash or two, long and curved like a goose neck or shaped and striped like the doublet of a medieval courtier. There is so much to buy here, so much to look at, so much to taste. A sign at the baker's stall, where you can acquire the hoop-shaped bread called *la couronne* or ask for a chunk to be cut from a loaf as big as a foot-stool, says that samples are not just free but "obligatory."

In Mirepoix, the *grand marché* takes place on the second and fourth Monday of every month. At *la foire*, on the first and third Monday, you can buy clothes as well: gaudy sweaters made of acrylic, embroidered tunics from North Africa and India, socks hand-knitted from local wool and boots and sandals of sturdy leather made by a craftsman who lives in the hills. The *friperie* man shows up with his bins of second-hand shirts and skirts to rummage through. On the hat stall are the flat caps, checked and plain, that all the older men wear, straw hats trimmed with fabric flowers and — for anyone who fancies himself as a *boulevardier* — straw boaters *à la* Maurice Chevalier. Another merchant sells the kind of functional underwear that diet-conscious societies elsewhere haven't seen in three generations: peach-coloured corsets, heavily banded, with garters pendant; massive pairs of knickers; brassieres capacious enough to house award-winning pumpkins, all laudable feats of engineering.

Late in the autumn, close to All Saints' Day, when it's traditional to place flowers on the graves of loved ones, the florists' stalls are awash with enormous plastic pots of chrysanthemums with white curved petals or petals of searing lemon yellow or a creamy russet red, the flowers so closely massed together that their greenery is almost invisible. In the summer the market square is the setting for antiques and crafts festivals and, each August, a celebration devoted to dolls and marionettes. But the liveliest events are those that celebrate the harvest.

Driving into Mirepoix on an October weekend on one of our first visits to the region, we heard sounds of revelry. We parked the car and tracked the noise to its source: a band of musicians in blue uniforms and black, wide-brimmed hats preceded a troupe of dancers in colourful regional costumes, many also masked. Following the parade into the square, we discovered the town celebrating chestnuts and the first wine of the season. Vin de Pays d'Oc Primeur read the label, its sharp yellows and greens as sprightly as the flavour of the Sauvignon Blanc and Chardonnay sold in generous glassfuls or, for the cost of a couple of glasses, by the bottle. At the centre of the square, men roasted chestnuts in flat wire-bottomed trays held over crackling wood fires, shaking the nuts from side to side, a two-person operation that released showers of orange sparks which rose into the cold blue sky before drifting back to earth like the aftermath of a firework. A trio of women wrapped the blistering hot chestnuts in paper cones and sold them to passersby.

Mirepoix was *en fête*. A merry-go-round spun delighted toddlers and pony rides were offered alongside the cathedral. There was candy floss (*barbe à papa* — father's beard) and a stall where you could win a prize if you could snag the rotating plastic ducks. Sharing the fire with the chestnut roasters were men cooking strips of pork and sausages which they then sold sandwiched in half a baguette and drizzled with ketchup and mustard, a treat to eat to the sound of the band while the masked dancers waltzed under the market's iron canopy.

Late in the autumn, Mirepoix's apple festival brings together what looks like the Ariège's entire crop. For the past few years, we have made a point of being in on the pre-production sessions in the main square. In preparation for the festivities, groups of elderly ladies chatter away at tables while they use rubber bands to attach apples to the wire frames that will hang from the arcades' huge beams and posts. Every store creates its own specialized tribute to apples: the pharmacy displays a hefty mushroom made entirely of *pommes*; the *tabac* has assembled an enormous apple pipe; the travel agent shows an apple airplane. This year, every tree in the marketplace was now an apple tree, its "crop" carefully tied to its branches. At the centre of the square stood a giant windmill made of apples, a bit of a comedown after last year's effort: an immense Eiffel Tower. But even that was dwarfed by the extravaganza of the following year, which featured two gargantuan turtle doves either side of a heart. Even the Buddha in the town's Chinese restaurant had an apple in his mouth. In this mainly agricultural area, it's fitting that the products of the earth should receive so much homage.

Employment around Mirepoix still centres on farming, but it wasn't always so. For hundreds of years the old Languedoc coloured and wove the fabric that clothed much of France. The red dyes of Montpellier, the woad that enriched Toulouse and the blue wool and silk of Nîmes all helped the region prosper. Some locales were famous for specific industries: Esperaza near Rennes-le-Château, for instance, was a major hat-making centre and now houses a museum of *chapeaux*. In a region where fabric-making goes back to Roman times, Lavelanet has a textile museum and a sadly dwindling handful of factories, all that remains since cheap imported fabrics arrived on the scene. In Laroque d'Olmes just to the north of Lavelanet, an old loom stands on a traffic island, yet another reminder of how important the interlocking of warp and woof once was.

Today it's individuals rather than industry that continue the tradition. Near Montségur is a farm where you can buy lustrous mohair sweaters in incandescent colours and surpassingly soft scarves knitted or woven from the wool of goats that graze in the neighbouring fields. On the main square in Mirepoix is an atelier where a mother and daughter knit, weave and stitch elaborate coats and jackets. These are for special occasions. For every day or table use, I like to forage through local *brocantes* and flea markets. On one memorable occasion I found five dinner napkins softened by many washings, each one checked red and green and stitched with "PM" — Peter's initials. But the vintage find I really cherish is a rack to hold kitchen cloths. A long oval of timeworn blue-and-white painted tin dating back to the late 1800s, it has the intended function of each cloth carefully spelled out above each of its four hooks: *mains, verres, couteaux, vaisselles.* Secured to the wall of our kitchen in Vancouver, it holds four checked towels. We use them sloppily, at random and not as decreed, but I like to imagine their original owner in Mirepoix carefully sorting her laundry and distributing her towels as the rack stipulated: one for hands, one for glasses, one for knives, one for dishes. Basic equipment for the table. Just add the food and the wine that flows in such abundance in the town marketplace, and dinner is complete.

We first tasted this dessert at La Maison de Blanquette in Limoux. It utilizes the fennel that, wild or cultivated, shows up in dishes right along the Mediterranean coast. Bring these treats out of the refrigerator as you serve the first course so they have time to come to room temperature.

CRÈME CATALANE

1 cup	whipping cream	250 mL
1 cup	whole milk	250 mL
2 tsp	fennel seeds	10 mL
1/2 tsp	vanilla essence	2.5 mL
	Finely grated zest of a lemon	
3 tbsp	sugar	45 mL
4	egg yolks	4

Mix cream, milk and fennel seeds in a saucepan and heat almost to boiling. Remove from heat and set aside for one hour.

Preheat oven to 325° F (165° C).

In a large bowl, mix vanilla and lemon rind. Strain milk-and-cream mixture into it and gradually add sugar. Whisk in egg yolks one at a time until mixture is light and frothy.

Pour into six 1/2-cup ramekins. Bake for 30 minutes or just until set. Refrigerate until an hour before serving time.

Serves 6

CHAPTER 11

Copper Pots and Cookbooks

DURFORT AND MONTOLIEU

"I don't care how much it weighs or what a nuisance it is to bring back," I said as we packed our cases for our umpteenth trip to the Languedoc. "I've read about this village where all they do is make copper cookware. We can drive there easily." I could see it on the stove, dark chunks of meat simmering in a winy sauce. "I've always wanted a big copper pot ..."

I t wasn't just the copper pot, it was the whole mystique of the French kitchen that we yearned for. If you're passionate about cooking and eating, it seems inevitable that at some point you must fantasize about having your own place in the French countryside. Renting different houses and visiting other people's, I was slowly collaging together in my mind's eye an imaginary home; though in hindsight it's revealing that I never even thought about bedrooms or a bathroom or the colour of the living room curtains or any other "decorator details."

Step outside the door, walk along the flagged pathway and you are in the *potager*, the kitchen garden with its battalions of lettuces, tomato plants and green spears of onions. In the kind of sunny spot where cats like to doze stand the terra cotta pots of herbs: the rosemary, the bay bush, the parsley. Each summer a vine provides a green canopy over the terrace. Inside, the *salon* is furnished with a long wooden table, already much scarred so that another small burn-mark from a casserole brought straight from the stove or a red crescent from the base of a wineglass only adds to the patina. The kitchen is as pictured in a dozen "lifestyle" magazines — except that it's real. The plaits of plump, papery garlic that hang from smoke-darkened beams are for use. A basket of onions stands on the table beside a bowl of freckled brown eggs and a pyramid of peaches on a flat, chipped dish. On the stove — wood-burning, naturally — a stew gently bubbles, its surface barely moving, sometimes in an iron pot blackened with age or, more photogenically (at least in my fantasy), in a copper pot, not shiny and polished but one that has acquired the speckles and shadings of regular use. Copper pots have always been inseparable from French cuisine for their ability to retain heat. When we heard there was a village that made nothing else within easy driving distance of the cottage we were staying in near Mirepoix, the opportunity was too good to miss.

In French, *dur* means hard and *fort* means strong: if a group of slick marketers had spent days in a think-tank session, they could not have come up with a better name than Durfort for a village known for centuries for its copperware. Conditions have improved mightily for coppersmiths since the days when they apprenticed at the age of thirteen and, in summer, worked as many hours every day. But the village has stayed much the same. Nestled into the steep, darkly forested hills of the Black Mountains, it's a network of narrow streets, their overhanging, half-timbered houses so well preserved that we felt we had mistakenly wandered onto a film set. Arriving minutes after twelve, we found all the *commerces* shut as tight as a lid on a casserole: the only vestige of life as we ambled around was the faint clatter of knives and forks through half-closed shutters — the usual French noontime symphony. We adjourned to a small patch of green near the river with a statue of the Virgin Mary and a water tap convenient for washing hands after a picnic of bread, cheese, grapes and a bar of evilly dark chocolate that flaunted its high cocoa content on the packet.

The artisans who work in Durfort are among the last in France to use techniques that date from the Renaissance. The river Sor that runs through the village created the industry, its power harnessed to drive a sledgehammer called a *martinet* which, guided by the coppersmith, shapes and distinctively dimples the copper. It is delicate, tiring work, positioning the metal with absolute precision in the short space of time that separates each blow of the hammer, guiding the energy that flows from river to tool to hand to copper vessel.

Durfort is a one-industry village. A huge copper vessel as tall as a man stands on the main street and shops that sell copper are everywhere. Some places carry nothing else while others, eyes on the tourist trade, also display brass- and pewterware and even lamps and china on their shelves. The copper ewers and warming pans we saw were strictly for decoration, hand-some "country" accessories intended to add an element of rusticity to a suburban villa or city apartment. But with cooking pots, utility comes first. Labels on some of the culinary pieces revealed a design and function unchanged in hundreds of years. Brought up from the cellar at the right season, a *bassine à confiture* was capacious enough to accommodate a lake of bubbling jam — or several fat ducks. An enormous kite-shaped *turbotière* was intended to hold an entire turbot (although the salesperson quickly pointed out I could also use it for other fish). Its size brought to mind images of fin-de-siècle banquets, of brigades of chefs, of Toulouse-Lautrec's stout, bearded *bon vivants* and their frilled and feathered ladies. More suited to modern kitchens were the small pans for sautéing, tall cylindrical pots intended for stock and saucepans in graduated sizes, little to large, hooked on their racks. Copper is a weighty metal, and what appear to be excessively long han-

dles provide the cook with the balance necessary to lift heavy brimming pots on and off a stove.

"We're enthusiastic cooks," I explained to the salesperson behind the counter in the Pierre Vergnes store. "Would it be possible to watch the process of manufacturing?" Absolutely, it was not a problem. She led us over to one corner of the store, not into a workshop but in front of a video monitor. The short documentary was a helpful introduction to the basic procedure but not the real thing. We asked again — could we see the actual *process* of shaping of copper? This time she escorted us outside and directed us to the atelier, a big, warehouse-like building just down the street.

Inside the high-ceilinged space, like oversized children on old-fashioned hobby horses, overalled workers sat astride metal poles worn smooth and shiny from repeated use, leaning against wooden backrests. I went over to watch their technique. At the end of the pole was a copper pot lid, which the coppersmith slowly rotated, shaping its rim with small taps from his hammer, the noise adding to the general cacophony. On the floor stood cauldrons and saucepans awaiting handles and the walls were lined with tools, huge metal pincers and hooks that looked like medieval instruments of torture. In the far corner, a workman ignited a burner on a stove and signalled us over. Flame roared. Taking a copper frying pan, he coated the inside with what looked like a dollop of grey sludge, then placed the pan over the heat. What followed was the kind of transformation that must have created murmurs of witchcraft in earlier times. In seconds, the interior became as dazzling as a mirror, plated with tin in a process called *étamage*.

Even with rigorous care these tin linings eventually wear away and require expensive refurbishment, and some present-day saucepans made of other materials perform almost as well as copper. Still, we were not dissuaded from staying true to tradition. For an hour or more, we talked to storekeepers about the merits of copper as a heat conductor, examined the thick-

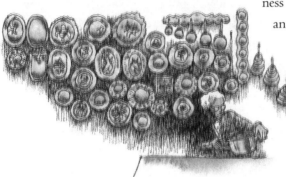

ness of tin linings (too thin and they erode quickly) and lifted pots by the ends of their handles to see how they felt in our hands. We probably scrutinized every saucepan in Durfort before we found the one we decided on. It was round, lidded and had two sturdy but essential handles — it would be weighty when it was filled with what we reckoned would be ragout enough for a dozen.

JUST AS OUR code word for Durfort is "copper town," Montolieu, just west of Carcassonne, is always simply "cookbook town" — though "book town" would be more accurate. Durfort's age-old industry means commerce more or less year round, but what happens if you are merely a typical French village with nothing especially noteworthy to offer? You reinvent yourself, as Montolieu has done. Its name — Mount Oliou in the language of Oc — alludes to the olive trees that were once grown in the area. But, like many villages in the Languedoc,

Montolieu's traditional industries, in this case textiles and wine-making, have eroded with time. Rather than dying, the pleasant and resourceful little village set itself the goal of becoming "the book capital of southern Europe."

Book villages and towns exist in Belgium, Japan, the U.S., Canada, Norway, Malaysia and the U.K., where the first one was started in 1961, part of a bibliophilic network that now has outposts all over the world. Montolieu joined the club in 1989, which means it was one of the first. What all these literary centres have in common is a rural, usually attractive location and — logically — an emphasis on books (new, second-hand and antiquarian), a magnet that typically draws bookbinders, calligraphers, printers, editors, translators and anyone else concerned with the written word to set up shop in the same community.

To avid readers, this is seduction beyond belief. One lifetime would not be sufficient to thoroughly plunder Montolieu's treasures, and the few hours we spend there whenever we can are never enough. Most stores seem to specialize in one type of book, though never exclusively. While the Librairie de Contrefort is a source of regional facts (I could spend days browsing through the information on Pyrenean flowers, history, travel, cooking and architecture), it also stocks the smallest books in the world, Guinness record-holders, each little more than a centimetre across, intended more as novelties than as serious reads. In a store called Alinéa, the owner tapped away at his keyboard while I wondered how I could ever dream up an excuse to write with a quill pen in ink that was violet in both colour and perfume. I riffled through a box of old sepia-hued postcards and, with the respect that I thought its age merited, carefully opened a two-volume *Grand Atlas de France*, full of engravings and almost too heavy to lift. These were for serious bibliophiles only, whereas Les Galeries des Bouquinistes, which occupied two floors of a large ramshackle building, stocked a bewildering selection broad enough to encompass books of *belles lettres* and rows of *romans policiers*: murder mysteries. In a nearby street, the window of Les Jardins d'Epicure displayed tales of classic adventure with faded poppy-red covers and turn-of-the-century graphics — "*L'Ile au Trésor*" and "*A la conquête du Pôle Nord*." Around them stood the wines of the region; the store inside was part library and part *cave* with books on one shelf and muscats and Minervois on the one below. A ripping yarn and a decent bottle is a happy combination indeed, but enough. While Peter went off with pencil and pad, I as usual was in search of words about food.

My understanding of French cannot always untangle the *argot* in a *roman policier*, but I can wander with reasonable ease through culinary techniques. *La Cuisine en Languedoc*, picked up in one of Montolieu's shops, was typical, a collection of time-honoured recipes of the kind that often omit quantities or timings, trusting that the user knows these from experience — most likely from watching while *maman* or *grandmère* made the same dish. I wondered to what extent this still happened in France knowing that, in North America, all that most children learned about cooking was how to open the door of a microwave. To be fair, women working outside the home don't have the time to make suppers from scratch every night, and I doubted whether even the most traditional of home cooks in France still made a dish called *sanquette* in which "*le sang du poulet*," the blood of a chicken, comes first in the list of ingredients (it's a kind of crêpe speckled with cubes of ham and topped with sprinkles of vinegar and chopped parsley; the blood stands in for the usual batter, making the dish essentially a large seasoned clot). Here too were instructions for *pain à la chichole* — slices of bread soaked in red wine and powdered with sugar. In omelettes, in tripe dishes, in a leg of lamb cooked with juniper berries, there was the inevitable *saindoux* — lard — standing in for the butter of the north. Dishes of river-caught fish; soups of utmost simplicity and economy; casseroles that utilized every last part of an animal. Digest their contents and, as elsewhere, you discover the recipes of a region reveal more of its flavour than any history book.

Bookstores are usually tranquil places that rarely arouse controversy but the sign outside L'Ile Lettrée is a deliberate provocation. On an upper storey, canted at a steep angle and aged by sun and rain, stands a tower of books impaled on a sword. "If you are a butcher, you put out a sign showing a cow. A fishmonger shows fish. Call my sign 'a brochette,'" said the store's proprietor, Daniel Olivier, with feigned innocence when I asked him for an explanation. His stock ranges from far right to the far left, from fascist to communist; Lenin and Trotsky are just inside the door. Known by the locals as *"M'sieu le diable,"* the devil himself, Olivier is a man who rolls his "r's" with demonic relish, laughs often and wildly, and publishes a newsletter shot through with appalling puns. But white-haired and wearing an Aran sweater and corduroy trousers, he looked more like a kindly grandfather than a subversive. In fact, there are piles of genteel magazines from the early 1900s farther back in the shop, whose scent is the friendly one of timeworn books, not brimstone.

The atmosphere was even more soothing in Des Livres et Vous, run by the handsome Stéphane Van Den Driessche, a

recent arrival from Belgium here to live out his dream. Initially he had filled his rented space with all kinds of literature, but now he was listening to input from his customers before deciding what areas to specialize in. He mostly bought his books in Brussels, although sometimes, he said, he borrowed a car and raided Carcassonne and Toulouse. Like most of Montolieu's storekeepers, his nose was often inside a book, currently T. E. Lawrence's *Seven Pillars of Wisdom*. Otherwise, he said, he played tennis every morning all year round. *La qualité de la vie.* That was why he had moved here from the rainy north.

Wasn't that, when you got to the core of it, what we were all after? A way of daily living that was simple, profound and real, linked to the seasons and the fruits of the earth. "Quality of life" is something both locals and transplants talk about all the time in the Languedoc; it's the holy grail that draws newcomers, many from other countries, to come here and put down permanent roots. The same seductive desire had already convinced us to live here for part of the year. Total neophytes, we shamelessly picked the brains of everyone we came in contact with. What were the steps involved in buying French property? What did you need to watch out for in terms of renovation? We got some help on this front from Ben, a young Englishman we met at a party in 1999 who invited us to come and see the house he had restored just west of the town of Foix.

Later that week, following his hand-drawn map, we forked off from the main highway onto what became a progressively narrower track along the rim of a hillside. We climbed gradually, the landscape falling away behind us, until we reached the end of the road and a cluster of farm buildings. Dogs barked, chickens scratched in the dirt, and the prospect of undulating hills and rolling pastureland was enough to take your breath away — or at least convince you, as it had Ben, to up stakes and say goodbye to your native land. "A view was paramount," he said as he told us the story of his search for a house to renovate, making the rounds of the notaries and estate agents every day for three months and picking up *09* (*Zéro Neuf*), a free weekly paper filled with classifieds whose cryptic shorthand he slowly learned to decipher.

It was an estate agent who finally drove him to a remote hamlet where almost the entire village, some five houses and barns, was for sale; for a while he entertained himself with thoughts of being lord of the manor, then realized that renovations on that scale take twenty years. Also for sale, but unadvertised, was a cottage on the commune's periphery. About 220 square metres and 150 years old, it was the largest house in the hamlet and belonged to an elderly farmer.

As we made our way through a big pot of *coq au vin*, Ben, Peter and I talked about the wisdom of buying houses in

various states of dilapidation. Seeking the benefits of insula-
tion and a well-sealed roof, Ben had been prepared to do a
complete renovation. "I wanted something that was as naked
as possible," he said, "something that hadn't been covered up."
His search had already taken him to vast farmhouses with no
toilet and no running hot water, so he was unfazed by the
single cold-water tap and rooms that were small by French
farmhouse standards: the bigger the rooms, he reasoned, the
harder they are to heat.

Preliminary impressions suggested that the house was falling
apart, but things that looked rotten weren't and the surprises
were mostly good ones. Underneath years of grime lay oak
floors, which he sanded and sealed with linseed oil. He attacked
the cement of the kitchen wall and unearthed fine beams hidden behind. The living room fireplace still had the traditional
pelmet of fabric around its right-angled mantel. It took seven-
teen rinses to get rid of the accumulated smoke of years.

We couldn't wait to get started. "You need vision and imagination," Ben told us, advising us that if we did find a place we
liked, we should not be swayed by first impressions. "Go and see
a place several times; I came up here three times a week for a
month." Experience with renovating Victorian townhouses in
England also allowed him to be clear-eyed about the work
required. "Most foreigners who are do-it-yourselfers make a
huge botch-up," he said. "Materials are different here." He had
learned to add a small amount of cement to lime mortar to stop
the birds and bees from stealing it, and that while some building materials (he cited porcelain shower bases) were cheaper in
France, paint was "ludicrously expensive." In its original state,
his farmhouse had had four bedrooms and only two windows;

opening up attics and a large shed had increased this to five bed-rooms plus a billiard room with a bar.

What was quickly becoming apparent was that if we did buy a house in the Languedoc, an extra bedroom was a necessity. In the time it takes for everyone at the table to eat dessert and sip a final coffee, mists can descend, throwing what looks like a grey mohair blanket across roads that even by day can be hair-raising. Often when we go to supper at Ben's or other friends we have made in the area, we take our duvet and toothbrushes along. Another British friend, Rob, lives within close dining range of a cottage we have rented several times near Camon, which genuinely is (as a sign proclaims) "one of the most beautiful villages in France." Where Ben has knocked down walls

to create a kitchen long enough to seat the dozens who came to celebrate his thirtieth birthday party, Rob and his wife built their house from the ground up using the post-and-beam technique, an architectural style unusual to the area.

Their exodus to the Languedoc in 1985 was partly prompted by, in Rob's words, "Thatcherism," and also by a shared dream of building a wood house. Other factors were the climate and the area, so close to the sea, so close to the mountains and so close to Spain. They found acreage on the top of a hill to park their mobile home and eventually, seduced by its views and sunsets, bought the land from their neighbour, an organic vegetable grower. Rob was a psychologist who had been involved in community buildings and Alison a linguist who, inspired by houses she had seen in North America, had decided to switch to woodwork; both were around thirty at the time. Up went the framing with wood from the nearby forest of Belesta. Down went floors of chestnut from a hundred kilometres away.

We learned all this over repeated coffees at the Café Castignolles in Mirepoix, and over supper one night at the cottage we had rented in nearby Léran. I served a soup made from local squash and a pasta with a ratatouille-inspired sauce of eggplants, zucchini, tomatoes and plenty of garlic. Living somewhere so unspoiled and natural makes you want to eat food that's the same, says Rob, a vegetarian who grows his own lettuces, carrots, tomatoes, cucumbers and other vegetables. "The older generation respects what you do with the land," he said when we dropped in to see him some days later, waving towards the broad plateau in front of their house. "In the Middle Ages, they tell me, jousts were staged here." We stood in the waning light, lost in thought, imagining the drama and the peace that this piece of land must have seen.

BY LATE OCTOBER, the highest and lowest temperature each day have stretched further and further apart, so that while it is still possible to take the baguette and cheese board outside at lunchtime, the chill slams down like a door as the shadows lengthen and dusk approaches. In the communal gardens in Camon, a few sodden tomatoes hang on stick-like stems but the kale is thrusting forth and the pumpkins are piled up like great orange beads on the market stalls. The lightness and ripeness of summer's fruit and vegetables gives way to sturdier fare: cabbages, potatoes, chestnuts. It is the time of year to make soup, and if you have a copper pot to do it in, so much the better.

The classic French coq au vin comes originally from Burgundy but versions show up all over the country. This is the recipe, named after his village, that our friend Ben often cooks on his wood-burning stove.

UROBECH COQ AU VIN

4	chicken legs, preferably free range	4
	Olive oil	
6 oz	smoked bacon cut into small "fingers"	180 g
2 lbs	leeks, finely chopped	1 kg
8 oz	mushrooms, coarsely chopped	250 g
1	bottle cheap red wine	1
2	capfuls brandy	2
1 cup	vegetable stock	250 mL
2 tsp	cornstarch	10 mL

Fry the chicken legs until golden brown in a large sauté pan, adding a little olive oil if needed. Remove chicken and add the bacon to same pan. Fry until slightly crispy, then set aside with chicken.

Cook the leeks in the remaining fat until soft and golden. Add the brandy "and flambé if you have an audience."

Add the bacon, chicken, chopped mushrooms and half the bottle of wine. Bring to the boil, add the stock, cover and simmer for 30 minutes, stirring occasionally and adding more wine to keep the sauce a liquid consistency.

Remove a quarter cup of the liquid and mix with cornstarch. Return the mixture to the pan and cook until thickened. Season to taste. Serve with rice or mashed potatoes and a green salad.

Serves 4

In October, market stalls are heaped with squash in all its vibrant colours and permutations. This autumnal idea for pumpkin soup comes from our friend Rob.

PUMPKIN SOUP

1/3 cup	butter	80 mL
1 1/2 lbs	pumpkin, peeled, seeded and cut into 1/2-inch (1.5-cm) cubes	750 g
1/2 tsp	nutmeg	2.5 mL
2/3 cup	milk	150 mL
1	bay leaf	1
2/3 cup	light cream	150 mL
	Salt and pepper	
	Homemade croutons	

Melt butter in a large pan. Toss pumpkin cubes with nutmeg, cover and cook gently until pumpkin is softened. Add the milk and purée with a hand blender. Add the bay leaf, cover pot and simmer for 10 minutes. Add the cream and bring just to boiling point.

Season to taste. Top with croutons.

Serves 4

CHAPTER 12

Foie Gras and Sanglier

LÉRAN AND COURTAULY

Philippe, the artisan who built the kitchen in our cottage, loves to eat. Because he's French, this means he also knows how to cook and how a kitchen should work. Which is why he constructed a small pull-out cabinet below the counter beside the stove. "For your oils, your vinegars," he said.

A h yes, the sherry and raspberry vinegars I splash liberally into pans to blend with the brown bits left behind when I sauté chicken. The walnut oil whose earthiness is so magically right in an arugula salad or with *lentilles du Puy*. As for those *lentilles*, it took me some time to get used to cooking in France where bottles and packages usually only sold in "gourmet stores" in North America are inexpensive enough to add without thought to the shopping cart.

"Don't we already have some dried *cèpes* in the cupboard?" said Peter one day as I reached for a jar in SuperU.

"No," I said. "We just have that *forestier* mix."

Keeping two kinds of dried fungi on hand wasn't wanton profligacy; it was the sheer delight of being able to stock the pantry and fridge with foods that qualify as treats for a special occasion elsewhere. Rounds and logs of fresh goat cheese, fir honey from the Pyrenees and, above all — so easy to find and so affordable — foie gras.

Pale, staggeringly rich and firm as cool butter, foie gras is the topmost pinnacle of gastronomic luxury. Its history dates back to the ancient Egyptians; the Romans fed their geese on figs to fatten them. In most parts of the world, the only places you can buy it are the very best restaurants and gourmet stores, but in our part of France it's everywhere. Each November, a local supermarket not far from Mirepoix features a *foire gras* (a fat fair!) where the "special of the week" is foie gras along with the chubby duck legs you need to make confit and the various other duck bits and pieces that result from the liver harvest. At other times we purchase the light buff foie gras at the Mirepoix market or by following hand-lettered roadside signs directing us to farmers who specialize in producing this ambrosial substance.

On our visit to their farm near Albi, the Rollands had told us how they made confit and showed us the little tripe rolls called *tripous* bobbing in their broth. The Rollands also produced foie gras, literally the "fat liver" produced when a goose or duck has a funnel put down its throat and is fed and fed and fed. "It's very important that the ducks don't suffer — or their livers aren't good," Paul Rolland had told us as we left the farmhouse and followed him towards some outbuildings. He pointed to a pond with pride and added with a laugh, "My farm is a Club Med for ducks!" Inside the barn, he poured a sample of the white maize that he feeds his flock for exactly fifteen days into my hand, so that I could see the pearly colour that would result in a desirably pale foie gras. As a dozen ducks stood unconcerned in a corner, Rolland let himself into their pen, separated one of the birds from its fellows, gripped it between his knees and seized my hand. "Come," he said to me, "see for yourself that the duck doesn't mind, put your finger down its throat." I did. It felt warm and slightly rough. The duck stood there with remarkable composure, showing no signs of alarm.

Some of the livers that come from these ducks are sold whole and at the Rollands' farm, medallions of the unutterably creamy substance are wrapped in duck meat or stuffed inside quail. For everyday eating, I go to the supermarket and buy tinned *bloc de foie gras*, the term for smaller pieces formed together, or *mousse de foie gras*, a sublime purée. One of the most opulent dishes you'll ever taste is potatoes fried in the fat left over from cooking a foie gras. Anywhere in the region, even the smallest leftover is used one way or another.

Chilly winters and a long-standing agricultural tradition go far to explain why the Languedoc is such a staunchly carnivorous region: you almost expect its map to be divided up like one of those charts that shows the cuts in a side of beef. From foie gras to confit to the skinny, spicy *merguez* sausages popularized by North African immigrants, meat plays a serious role in the cuisine here. Even so, it's unusual to find a restaurant that serves nothing else, and even rarer to come upon a place with no sign outside. It did acquire one in 1998, but the first time we ventured to the Auberge du Moulin de Patris, a restaurant we had heard much talk about, we seriously wondered if we had taken a wrong turn.

A long, rambling house with an attached barn at one end, the auberge is set back from a country road that meanders across the fields between the villages of Léran and Belloc, just south of Mirepoix. As we drove up on a gleaming autumn day, two hounds, tails wagging, bounded out to meet us and led us towards the entrance. Nothing suggested this was a restaurant, except for a glimpse of linen-set tables through a window. The front door was open so we walked in, called out a *bonjour* and, in a room leading off the hallway, found a couple watching television. "Talk to *mon fils*," the woman replied when I explained that we wanted to make a dinner reservation. A tall charming man in his late thirties, André Barthez was the essence of bonhomie, greeting us as though we were already the *amis* we would later become. Yes indeed, he told us, the restaurant was known for its specialties, foie gras and duck cooked over the wood fire. And that was it essentially. He named a price that seemed more than reasonable and we reserved a table for later in the week. Friends on holiday near Béziers were coming to spend a day or so with us. Why not share the experience? A restaurant that serves just two dishes and has no need to advertise was bound to be worth trying.

Two nights later, the car crunched across the gravel and, alerted by the barking dogs, André Barthez came out to greet us. The night was cold but the restaurant immediately embraced us with a warmth that was as much emotional as physical. Landscapes, still lives, and a child's drawing decorated the walls, rush-bottomed chairs were tucked under tables set with floral-patterned plates and a wood fire blazed in a corner. We clustered around the hearth as André told us the *moulin's* history. Built in the 1840s, the mill had been in operation until sometime after World War I; he pointed to a huge millstone embedded in the floor. His parents bought the mill, then in ruins, and converted it into their home, and a restaurant which they opened in 1970. Then he led us to our table.

First came the foie gras. We had ordered it both ways, *mi-cuit* and *frais*, accompanied by glasses of the local alternative to the more usual Sauternes, 1986 Rivesaltes, golden and sweet. Thick tranches arrived on a bed of frisée and with them bread, salt and pepper. Try both types of foie gras, said André, and see which you prefer. One was a honey colour, the other pinker, reflections of the diet the ducks had been fed during their *gavage*. Both were exquisite, like buttery satin. A bite of one, a sliver from the other, we couldn't agree which we preferred but, even though we ate like pigs, the serving was so bountiful that we could finish less than half of it. Next came a salad drizzled with shallot vinaigrette, its tomatoes sliced almost to transparency, each slice so thin you could fold it in half with your fork, its freshness a welcome interlude. The duck *magret* (its steak-like breast) was cooked on the grill, crisp outside and pink-rare inside, juicy, tender and tasting of woodsmoke. Two of us chose confit which, served in an oval pottery dish, fell off the bone at the touch of a fork into a sauce of swarthy mushrooms tasting earthily of the forest floor. With both dishes came blistering hot *frites* and, afterwards, a small green salad from the garden. Dessert was a simple choice of sorbets with a matching liqueur as sauce: pear with poire William; raspberry with framboise. Impeccable French logic at work.

Now it was time to leave. Take the rest of the foie gras with you, André had said at some point in the evening, but in our enthusiasm over the remainder of dinner, we forgot. Darn, I thought, the following day, the mere notion of leftover foie gras … The next night, as I began to whisk eggs for an omelette, mourning what we had left behind, there was a knock on the door and there stood André with a foil-wrapped parcel. At some point we had told him we were staying in a *gîte*, no more, but he had gone to the trouble of finding out where we were. Come in, join us for an aperitif. There is no better glue than food to bind a friendship, and no more powerful motivation to start one.

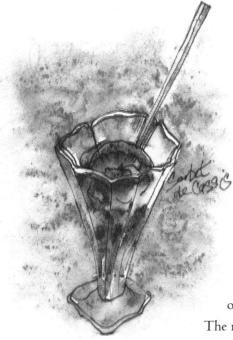

Ingredients and their source. At the Rollands' farm near Albi, we had seen foie gras "on the hoof" but if I wanted to learn the intricacies of its preparation, the Moulin de Patris was obviously the place to spend time. The next afternoon, I walked down to the phone box beside the post office and called the restaurant. Could we come over and talk, I asked? Of course.

For the first few years that Denise Barthez, André's mother, and Vincent, his father (who died in 1999), ran the restaurant, they offered a broader menu. Round about 1973, they whittled it down to its current simplicity. "This is why people come here," said André as we sat with him and Denise in her cozy tiled kitchen, and why he is meticulous about his foie gras sources. Rather than buying from an individual farm where, he says, the quality may not be consistent, André obtains his supply from a wholesaler, a couple who sell from their home. That way he can personally select each liver, basing his choice on colour and firmness but not necessarily size (a typical foie gras weighs 600 grams). The livers come from the Gers *département* in summer and from the Ariège in the cooler months. He removed one from the refrigerator. "Touch it," he said. "It's sweet in your fingers," adding, "you also choose with your nose."

Foie gras served *frais* is uncooked, just cleaned, then liberally salted and peppered, wrapped in foil and refrigerated for a day. *Mi-cuit* involves a long slow bath in barely simmering salt water. Prepared this way and covered with duck fat, a foie gras will keep under refrigeration for three weeks. André gets his *magrets* and duck legs from the same supplier: "A duck that gives good foie gras, gives good meat." He serves his foie gras with salt, pepper and bread, nothing else. If customers ask, it can be cooked in a pan with vinegar, or with butter, apple and Calvados, although "it's not possible to eat as much foie gras when it's hot." It can also be cooked in Armagnac or port or with truffles, he shrugged, "But why would you when the foie gras itself is so good?"

The confit we had eaten at the restaurant, we learned, wasn't really traditional confit, the duck treated with salt first, then cooked for an hour or so, *frémissement* (shivering) in its own fat. André makes his confit once a week from duck legs that are gently warmed in a large pot until the fat melts away, then cooked over the fire with onions until they are bronzed. The next step depends upon the season. It was September, so André was adding fresh tomatoes from the garden. In spring, it might be locally foraged wild mushrooms — *mousserons de St. Georges, morilles,* or *trompettes des morts.* In the winter, he sometimes makes the family version of cassoulet at the back of the fire, filling the *toupi* (an Occitan word for cooking pot) with beans and confit and adding a pig's feet, shin and a sausage made with its skin. The cooking takes a full day.

Regulars come every four to six weeks to the Moulin de Patris, and this is where locals bring guests from Paris or Toulouse. "After so many years, people would be very disappointed if we did anything else," says André of his minimalist menu.

Our friendship hinged on pure chance. If we had not mentioned that we were staying in the village, André would never have known where to deliver the leftover foie gras. Had we been staying in a hotel, we might have already journeyed on and never seen him again. Which is another reason we were finding it judicious to base ourselves for weeks at a time in rented cottages, where we could invite friends, old or new, in for a muscat or a meal. And to anyone who lives to eat, the chance to cook French dishes that are unquestionably authentic is too tempting to pass up. Wandering around any market is slow torture if you cannot buy the ingredients. Having my own, albeit temporary, kitchen lets me ask the butcher for a kilo of the muscular bourgignon cut of beef to simmer for hours with red wine and onions, permeating the place with delicious smells; or pick up a big bag of scarlet peppers to grill and skin (their uses are legion); or take home a packet of authentic *lentilles du Puy* to make a rustic salad heady with walnut oil.

The year we met André, we were staying in a small *gîte* in Léran. Back in the summer in Canada, we had signed and returned the complex form and received a sketch of the house and the address of the owner's parents, keepers of the keys. Apart from its location, on a side road midway between Mirepoix and Lavelanet, we knew little about the village, but we liked it on sight, its main street lined with honeyed stone houses and plane trees whose patchy bark, olive green, brown and khaki, always reminds me of paint-by-numbers kits. As promised, the *gîte* was definitely *mignon* (sweet), with a spacious downstairs room that combined kitchen, dining and living areas with an adjacent shower room. Upstairs were two bedrooms snugly tucked under the eaves; we were constantly banging our heads. But what did that matter when you could pull aside the lace curtains and look out across the treetops to the turreted château, or listen to the sound of the river from the surprisingly large back garden?

By now, we were old hands at dealing with the vagaries of other people's homes. The same year we had not bought the impractical house with the turret, a mutual friend had introduced us by phone to Mark, an American journalist living in a village of seventy people, who had purchased a colossal barn some years earlier and was slowly renovating it while contributing stories, via e-mail, to newspapers on two continents. The cottage we borrowed from him was attached to the end of his barn and ideal for the three of us (we had brought Kate plus her schoolbooks along). Its small flagstoned terrace faced the village

Wild *Garlic* · *Quarante, France*
Peter Matthews

square where a fountain, home
to goldfish and geckoes, burbled, watched by the
elderly mayor, who sat outside his *mairie* most of the day on a
wooden chair. If we left the door open, as we invariably did,
village dogs wandered in and out. A few times a week, a peremp-
tory "parp, parp" signalled the arrival of the travelling butcher's
van. Soon after, aromas of garlic, onions and meat percolated
out of windows shuttered against the sun, followed not long
after by the metallic music of cutlery.

While Peter painted and Kate went off exploring, I would often go for a walk in the meadow up behind the barn, its poppies drops of pure scarlet, the only sounds the muted chatter of birds and the whoosh of the wind through the trees. A flotilla of tiny blue butterflies escorted me like drifting flakes of sky. It was at times like these that I thought more and more about what it would be like to live — and cook — here for months at a time.

The *gîte* in Léran had the same kitchen facilities as a standard village house: four gas burners fuelled by a propane tank and a small oven with, to anyone not French, ambiguous controls. Trusting to luck the first night we were there, I slid a yellow-skinned chicken stuffed with a branch of thyme picked from the roadside into the oven. The bird puffed up, its skin golden-brown and taut, and I thickened its juices with crème fraîche to make a sauce. Next came a salad with most of a baguette, then some sloppy Camembert and the remaining bread, followed by equally juicy pears. Welcome to France. The next night, I simmered what was left of the bird in red wine with mushrooms and chopped onions and steamed a pot of potatoes to mash (with a little more crème fraîche) to sop up the sauce. The following evening, using the Mouli I found in a drawer, I puréed a smooth leek-and-potato soup whose base was stock from the chicken bones.

We liked Léran considerably. Its only "tourist attraction" is the pepperpot-turreted château once owned by the Duke of Mirepoix, now turned into elegant private apartments. Beyond it, full of flickering sunlight, is a tunnel of plane trees. In the other direction lies Montbel Lake, a pleasant walk after a hefty lunch. And having André Barthez and his restaurant so close by was no hardship. Ah, that leftover foie gras. Even spread lavishly on chunks of baguette as an immoderately greedy hors d'oeuvre, what he had brought us lasted three evenings. Several times we stopped in at the Moulin de Patris to say "hello," and invariably talk leaned towards food. Come, said André one afternoon, and he invited us to his house to meet Corinne, his wife, and his children Paul and Lisa; and also (and I think this could only happen in France) to see the woodcock he had shot a day earlier.

We sat around sipping coffee in the farmhouse on the hill before adjourning to the kitchen to view the bird. After it is plucked, it is not gutted, André said. We hang it from a hook in the fireplace by a string, over bread spread with foie gras; the bird's juices drip onto this as it cooks and form a cherished component of the meal. If he has several woodcocks he invites friends around to sit and tell hunting tales and drink good wine. (Whether these gatherings feature the lusty toast that André proposed on one occasion, I do not know: "*à nos femmes, à nos chevaux, et à ceux qui les montent,*" he said as he raised his glass. Discretion forbids translation.)

In this part of France, *la chasse* focuses on the quest for the ultimate edible, provender for the winter that lies ahead: *sangliers* — wild boar. Every Wednesday and weekend through the autumn, we saw cars parked by the roadside and hunters in brown and green camouflage heading into the forests, and heard the dull thud of guns and the gulping bark of dogs. *Sangliers* are said to be shy creatures, and the one I came upon one fine afternoon in the woods near Montségur was certainly as startled as I was. Grey and bristly, about the size of a fully-grown golden retriever, it froze on the spot before charging off through the trees.

The next *sangliers* I saw were far more sedate. At some point, one of us had circled the name Courtauly on our yellow Michelin map. Neither of us could remember why, so we drove there one fine Saturday and discovered a tranquil and pretty village. We parked, ambled around, noticed a house for sale, peered through the window and made out a huge fireplace, wandered on, exchanged *bonjours* with a man we met in the street and commented on the beauty of the afternoon and the village. "Would you like to see a *sanglier*?" he asked. A strange non sequitur of a question, but certainly, we would. Penned, we assumed. He led the way. "*Deux sangliers,*" he elaborated over his shoulder as we followed him up the street to a barn and allowed him to steer us inside. "*Ils sont morts,*" he added, superfluously by then. On the floor lay two very large and very dead wild boars. We shook hands with the hunters, men in their middle to late years attired in hunting gear, traditional French "blues" and checked shirts. We met the mayor, a man of quiet friendliness and dignity. We regretted that we had not brought the flash to take photographs, we said. No matter. He and his friends lugged the creatures outside and posed proudly in the sunshine.

A truck pulled up. The man with the scale had arrived. The larger of the boars was hefted on and proved to be a massive 110 kilos. Big, but not as big as the biggest around, said one hunter; that had tipped the scales at 140. By now, we had become *"les amis,"* and we must be given some *sanglier* to taste for ourselves. Peter, whose stomach is weaker than mine, disappeared as the boars were pulled into the barn and the butchering began. Each animal was set in a V-shaped wooden trough, its skin flayed to reveal maroon muscle and a white layer of fat. The first boar was hung up by its heels from a metal hook in the ceiling, its blood drained and hosed away. The butcher moved in and gutted it, setting the liver and heart aside and throwing the remainder into buckets to be saved for the dogs. The smell was hot, metallic and heavy, the scene bloody, but there was an almost balletic precision to the ritual and to the skill and cooperation of the hunters. As one held a hoof while another wielded a knife against skin held taut by a third, I had the feeling that they had done this many times before.

By now the smaller boar had been removed from its hook, the tendons securing it cut with a single stroke of the knife and its carcass sawn neatly in half. With advice and input from the hunters, the butcher excised a long piece of meat, the kidney attached, cut and trimmed it carefully, then handed it to me, still warm, in a green plastic bag. Marinated with red wine, herbs and juniper berries for several days, it made a memorable and very gamy ragout.

Hunting in France is different from hunting in North America. What motivates *les chasseurs* here is the pursuit of flavour — the flavour you can only get in an animal that has fed on acorns and whatever else it finds on the forest floor. What drove this home was seeing hunting magazines in the *presse* in Mirepoix. As well as articles on fish, fowl and animals, they included information on foraging for mushrooms and which wild berries were worth looking for. It was the opposite of the macho killing of a moose to display its head on your rec room wall. These hunters weren't after trophies, they were on a food safari.

My improvised recipe paled beside the wild boar we ate on a subsequent visit when André and Corinne invited us to dinner. The rain was barrelling down as we drove up the track to their farmhouse, oblongs of light at the windows like welcoming beacons. Inside it was unutterably cozy, the logs sputtering and crackling in the huge open fireplace, a leggy pointer dog curled up in a basket it shared amicably with a cat. Over the fire, suspended by the same tough white string used to tie sausages, a huge piece of meat rotated slowly, an entire leg of *sanglier* weighing about six kilograms and dark from its twenty-four-hour marinade in red wine, leeks, onions and shallots. "Juniper is an option," said André as he swabbed the meat with marinade and olive oil, "but I used cloves instead." It would take about three and a half hours to cook, he reckoned.

As we settled back on the deep sofa with our aperitifs and ate slices of Serano — Spanish ham that he had bought in Andorra — conversation turned to the various names that are given to the same cut of different animals: *gigot* for leg of lamb, *cuisseau* for deer, *jambon* for pigs and boars. Out came olives stuffed with anchovies, a salty counterpoint to the same Rivesaltes 1986 that we had sipped on our first visit. Nine of us, relatives and friends, sat down to dinner with a first course of beige-pink foie gras, a whole one, which Denise had sliced into neat pieces with the skill of someone who has cut up many a foie gras in her time. We spread it on bread and drank more Rivesaltes. André disappeared into the kitchen to carve long slices of *sanglier*, arranging them in an earthenware *tian*, a round, shallow, straight-sided dish. He cut and served one especially tender section of boar called *la souris* — the mouse — separately. Reduced, strained and with a little dark chocolate and honey added, the marinade made an intense sauce, almost medieval in taste. Apples and quinces, sautéed with butter in separate pans, were a distinct contrast to the heftily-flavoured meat, and then Corinne's father, the jovial bearded Roger, served cheese and more red wine. Dessert was ice cream topped with a homemade conserve of figs and a long loaf of *pain d'épices* — gingerbread. It was a dinner, like the friendship that drew the table together, that was *authentique* in the very best sense of the word.

Outside France, fresh foie gras and wild boar aren't that easy to find. Still, you can re-create an authentic French dessert. This is Corinne Barthez's recipe for the gingerbread that she served us that night at their farmhouse. Moist and dense, it's delicious topped with homemade preserves, softly whipped cream or vanilla ice cream.

CORINNE'S PAIN D'ÉPICES

1/2 cup	butter	125 g
3/4 cup	honey	200 g

1/2 cup	sugar	125 g
1 packet	dried yeast	11 g
1/4 cup	milk	50 mL
1 cup	flour	250 mL
3	eggs	3
1 tbsp	fennel seeds	15 mL
1 tbsp	ground cinnamon	15 mL
2 tsp	ground ginger	10 mL
2 tsp	orange flower water	10 mL
	Pinch of salt	

Preheat oven to 350° F (175° C)

Cut the butter into cubes, add the honey, and melt the two together in a bain-marie or microwave. Add sugar and beat the mixture with a wooden spoon.

Dissolve the yeast in the milk. Add to the butter mixture and mix.

Mix in all other ingredients. Pour into a non-stick loaf pan.

Bake for 40 minutes.

CHAPTER 13

Baguettes and Patisserie

CHALABRE
AND THE HOUSE-HUNT

The books, brochures, postcards and village announcements that I've brought back over the years now fill several shelves. Ephemera? Memorabilia? I'm not sure what the correct term is for the thin sheets of paper printed with charming, old-fashioned drawings of brioches and croissants that boulangers wrap around their baguettes. I only wish I'd had the foresight to write details about the meal or the day on the back of every one.

Right from our very first visit to the Languedoc in 1993 we got into the habit of the early morning croissant run. Early one morning, I walked down from *le petit château* in Chalabre not just to buy breakfast but also to see how events were progressing. We'd noticed the ROUTE BARRÉE sign the previous evening at the end of the main street. It was May, merry month of *fêtes* and festivals, and the carnival was coming to town. Normally it was peaceful this early in the morning, the only sounds the swish of a broom as a woman swept the sidewalk or the occasional noise like ripping taffeta as a moped tore through the village, but today clattering, hammering and shouts showed that work was well underway. It was a snug fit, shoehorning a full-blown carnival into a street of average width, and by the time the workmen had finished there was little more than a metre between the sideshows and the houses on either side.

That night, bouncing with excitement, all the children in the community assembled inside the *mairie* (town hall), emerging in an orderly line, each holding aloft a paper lantern, pausing as they exited so that *maman* or *papa* could click their disposable lighter and ignite the candle inside. Holding their lanterns ahead of them with huge care, they joined the village procession, scarlet globes bobbing through the crowd like fishing floats. Along the street, flashing lights illuminated the bumper cars and the booths where you could throw darts at balloons or shoot at targets to win plaster models of John Wayne and plush toys the colours of cheap candy. Even the housebound were part of the *fête*; opened shutters revealed usually private living rooms, many the site of impromptu celebrations.

A Languedoc community has a shape to it that I have come to love. It's like the mechanism of a giant clock, its wheels intermeshing, counting off the annual rituals of harvest and fair, the weekly markets and the dependable comforts of daily routine, beginning with bread on the breakfast table. Every morning in Chalabre on that first trip, one of us would rise soon after seven, let themselves quietly outside and walk across the bridge and along to the bakery to buy still-warm croissants. Often you'd pass other villagers returning home with their paper bags or baguettes,

but the day I got up at 5 a.m. to go and watch Pierre Vergé make his morning's supply, the village was sound asleep, silent except for a chorus of birds. Apart from a handful of street lamps, the only sign of life was the long chute of light that spilled from the bakery window. I tapped gently on the glass and, just as I thought Pierre had forgotten our rendez-vous, I spotted his shadow. He clicked the door open, wiping his fingers on his blue apron before shaking hands, and motioned me to follow him behind the counter into the white-tiled bakery.

He was already at work, sliding the big flat rectangle of dough he had made the previous evening through the rolling machine, a move that sealed in its butter and flattened the dough still further. He flung handfuls of flour onto a big marble board and spread the dough out on it, his short sleeves revealing arms made muscular from twelve years of rolling. When the dough was to his liking, he cut it down the middle with a single stroke, then evened the edges before slicing half the dough from top to bottom in a series of quick strokes. On each little rectangle he set small logs of chocolate, one at the top, one in the middle, then neatly rolled them up. Voilà! *Pains au chocolat.*

Pierre cut the remaining dough into triangles, then made a small slash at the broad end of each and, in four practised movements — one to separate the dough from the marble, the second to spread the slash slightly, the third to roll up the dough, the last to curve it into the classic crescent shape — turned it into a croissant. While the croissants rose on their parchment-covered tray, he made bread, a mellow hum filling the air as the mixer swung the dough, now slower, now faster, around and around on the end of its massive hook.

Birdsong came in through the open window.

A timer's "ping" informed him that it was time to start assembling his daily batch of chocolate croissants. But first Pierre scooped out small pieces of stiff hazelnut paste from a plastic container. *Noisette* (which these were), chocolate or plain, whatever the croissant type, he said, its tip is always tucked under so that it cannot come loose during the baking. The church clock struck six. Outside the night was still black but his work was only beginning. Pierre scraped off the marble counter and formed the dough into loaves of *pain de campagne*, cutting and weighing each one, adding or removing small pieces to make up the required 300 grams. Then, tucking each loaf into a compact ball, he flattened it with the heel of his hand, rolling it in a circular motion on the flour-strewn surface before folding it in half and placing the now oval ball of dough on the counter with the seam side underneath.

Outside, the sky was slowly turning a dark indigo blue.

Next he rolled each loaf with his hands, slowly moving them apart to taper the ends: the bread bulged in the middle like a recently fed boa constrictor. Two long slightly diagonal gashes with a razor blade set in a holder, and the bread was ready to rise. On their rack, the croissants were beginning to puff up. Meanwhile, there were still the day's pastries to be made. In a process that took no more than a minute, Pierre greased a metal ring, passed a batch of pastry dough through the rolling machine, flattened it further with his rolling pin and used his thumbs to press the pastry firmly against the inside walls of the ring, to be baked "blind" (empty) for a *tarte aux fruits*: of whatever's in season, he said: strawberries, kiwi, raspberries ... From the remaining pastry, he cut circles that he punctured with a spiky wooden roller, building blocks for a Black Forest cake. Finally he brought out a container of pears from the fridge, already peeled and sliced into perfect half-moons, and arranged them carefully in a pastry case he had made earlier.

I looked through the window. It was light outside. This was happening in villages all over France this very minute, I thought. Everyone, from the most impoverished tramp to the grandest château owner, could rise and head for the *boulangerie* to buy properly baked bread at a minimal price. Here, it was a staple of life; outside of France it had become a status symbol.

Pierre wiped down the work surfaces and covered the rolling machine with a red-and-white checked cloth. Now it was time to paint the croissants with a glossy coat of beaten egg. Done ... with the speed of long practice. Then a gust of hot air filled the room as he opened the oven door and slid half the trays inside. Three more minutes and in went the remaining trays. While they baked, Pierre cut discs from a sheet of already-prepared *génoise* (sponge cake), piecing the leftovers neatly together: more layers for the Black Forest cake. At 7 a.m., half the croissants came out of the oven with a zephyr of steam and a smell of butter and, a few minutes later, the rest of this morning's batch. In their place went the *tartes aux poires*, the pastry discs and the shell. Outside the sky was deepest blue. "*Fini,*" said Pierre. Soon his first customers would be arriving. He has each afternoon off but otherwise he works all day, shaping roses and leaves out of almond paste for a birthday cake or creating bonbons shaped like ripe chestnuts, the brown nut visible through the crack in its green marzipan coating. The day ends at 7:30 p.m., when the last person comes in to collect a loaf for supper or a *tarte* ordered earlier.

A decade later, we had our own *boulangerie* to go to for croissants and, finally, we had our own home in the Languedoc. Putting the key in our new front door for the first time, we thought back on what had been a long, frustrating but sometimes humorous journey. We had come to appreciate the endless patience of the *immobiliers* who showed us houses. So many houses. With its small square tower, one place we investigated looked promising from the outside. Greeting us at the door, its owners, a tidy couple built like salt and pepper shakers, were glowingly proud of their extensive renovations: the tiled floors of each room, each one a different colour, the granite-covered staircase so smooth and shiny ("it's like French gravestones," Peter whispered) and the many, many alcoves and niches for knick-knacks. And, as they made a point of telling us, the pale pink melamine-covered kitchen cupboards with which they had replaced the wooden ones — very old, they stressed — were included in the asking price. The wonderful garden almost made us overlook all the work it would take to return the house to its original condition. Spacious, marked out in vegetable beds, it led to a trail that ended at the dark smudge of a forest, a reliable source, said the owner, of *champignons* and escargots. As for the spectacular view of the Pyrenees, to see the sun set over the trees ... We sighed in unison. The fog had settled into an impenetrable greyness, and what sun there was was invisible. "It's too ... too renovated," we muttered as we drove away in the agent's car.

If this first house leaned too far in one direction, the second one was the opposite. Perhaps the agent was establishing benchmarks, we thought, as he escorted us into a place in drastic need of help — and money. Jerry-rigged electric wiring looped along walls and across ceilings. Floorboards had a scary sponginess to them. One wall had an enormous hole.

Over the years, house-hunting became an ongoing, but admittedly never full-time, project. We viewed partly renovated houses whose owners had given up in despair, among them an *ancien* home that belonged to a British couple who had spent every summer holiday for a decade slaving away at repairs. We could track their downward emotional spiral, the ceiling incision that revealed rotting beams, the exploratory holes in the wall that only uncovered more decay, the bath that had sunk through the floor. They hadn't even got around to working on the shop next door that was included in the understandably modest asking price.

Space was sometimes the problem — not too little, but too much. One community was eager to sell a house so massive that its rooms were large enough to accommodate evening classes in silk painting and, to judge from the rows of chairs and desks and the samples pinned to the wall, obviously did. Two streets

away the owners of a much smaller property had received a sudden windfall, which prompted them to install a bathroom at last. There it stood in all its turquoise glory — at one end of the garage. Elsewhere we slithered across enormous floors of pink Spanish marble so extravagant that they had forced the owner into bankruptcy. In another house in another town, we tried to pretend that the view was in no way devalued by the rear of a supermarket that blocked most of it, and in yet another to believe the agent when he pointed to an expanse of cement large enough for a jetliner to land on and said, "It would be easy to remove and make a garden."

On a solo trip, Peter phoned me excitedly. "There's a medieval château for sale, *a château!*"

It was only slightly beyond our absolute maximum price range but my vision of myself as a chatelaine died fast. He called the following day, considerably less elated, to report that the chill damp that permeated the many rooms was also authentically medieval and that arrow slits, while photogenic, made for a paucity of light only a bat could love. On occasion, we even came close to buying somewhere on pure emotion. Both of us yearned to find a cottage in the village of Carla de Roquefort (a name so evocative I've thought of using it as a pen name) and we would have been just as content, for the same reason, to live in Troye d'Ariège. Together Carla and Troye sounded like the stars of a tempestuous French movie. I would have been gratified to have either of those names allied to mine on a thin blue airmail envelope.

In yet another house, a remarkably sanguine real estate agent didn't attempt to hurry us by the frieze of furry mould that climbed a foot up the walls: "A little problem with the damp," he acknowledged. But while agents could be beguilingly honest, photos could lie. Carefully cropped out of snapshots was a landmark visible for miles around, right next to the picturesque seventeenth-century presbytery we had driven for hours to see. A grain silo? An integral part of the French electricity system? We still don't know. Another time, a house we found on the Internet looked, in pixels at least, like a miniature Buckingham Palace with a balcony, railings and tall windows. But its back

façade was mostly concrete and you could have reached from
one window and touched the supermarket across the street.

We didn't have the right vocabulary either when, on our first
house-hunting trip, we specified *une maison de village*. We quickly
discovered that a house in the heart of a small French community rarely comes with a garden, often faces right onto the main
(and only) street and is socketed into its neighbours like a piece
in a jigsaw puzzle. One person we met told us of punching a
hole in his living room wall only to find he had just opened a
window into the bedroom of a neighbour; fortunately the good
man said nothing, though shortly afterwards he hung a painting
over the peephole.

Bilingualism works both ways, of course. As potential pur-
chasers, we needed the right words to explain why a house, the
seventh today that an agent had shown us, wasn't precisely right.
We mastered the French for, "it's not exactly to our taste,"
an umbrella expression that left everyone feeling comfortable.
"Too big" was one graceful way out, as was "too small," but the
kindest response we evolved as we attempted to think of the
words for "I know it's a house with a view, which is what we said
we wanted, but ..." was to exclaim that this house had *beaucoup de
possibilités*. For decoration, for expansion, for launching a cooking
school. Let him infer whatever he liked — except the possibility that we wanted to make an offer.

On the other hand, there was an honesty about French home-
buying that we came to appreciate. There are no fulsome adjec-
tives, no advertisements promising "darling cutie waiting for your
TLC," and the concept of "open houses" with lamps lit, cookies
baking and kids hid — all that spurious set-dressing — doesn't
exist. *Au contraire*, French people are remarkably open about showing

you how they live. In dimly lit windowless rooms we tripped over cats, knocked over coffee cups and came upon occupants in their pyjamas avidly watching American sitcoms. Conversely, if a house is empty, it's empty, with the electricity switched off; competent French real estate agents all carry flashlights. The most unnerving houses to roam around in were those in the twilight zone where the owner had already moved to be with his sister in Toulouse or his son in Marseilles but, like the crew of the *Marie Celeste*, left his possessions behind. Once I whisked back a curtain to reveal a row of single shoes; as I stared, a prosthetic leg slid from the shadows onto the floor. We didn't buy that one either.

We must have been a real estate agent's worst nightmare. But at least seeing what we didn't want was teaching us the musts: a *boulangerie* down the street, a place that wasn't overpopulated by weekenders, church bells that not only told the time but would inform us of occasions for rejoicing or solemnity. And in the end we found it.

It's over a decade since that first night when Peter and I resolved to visit Carcassonne. Much has changed in this land we've come to love so much: André closed the Moulin du Patris — but we still eat foie gras and duck at his home or ours. Pierre the baker left Chalabre long ago, the hotel by Marseillan harbour is closed, a favourite cassoulet shop in Castelnaudary has changed hands. And technology has brought us closer. Where we used to keep in touch with newfound friends through occasional letters, we now send regular e-mails. Websites tell us what the weather is like in Perpignan and a webcam takes us to Collioure's harbour any hour we want it to. But by and large, the differences we notice each time we return are more evolutionary than revolutionary: another film of tobacco smoke

enriches the amber walls of the Café Castignolles in Mirepoix and now, each market day, a girl — a modern troubadour — plays a flute in the square. These changes only add layers to what was already there. People come, people go, but what is real, *authentique*, remains the same. Each visit makes me question more and more how the French remain so closely linked to their table. I hear our neighbours discuss the finer points of the cassoulet that Josette has just made for us. We realize that the institution of Sunday lunch is not the same as brunch in a restaurant.

The annual crop of garlic and strawberries and cherries gives way to the mushrooms, the chestnuts, the new wine. The light and shade washes over the walls of Montségur as it has for centuries. The disturbing contrast of brutal history and benign landscape remains.

The hot sun.

The cool shadow.

After a hearty casserole, or confit of duck with red cabbage, and after the cheese board has been taken away, this is one of our favourite ways to end a dinner.

PEARS IN RED WINE

Six ripe but not too soft pears with stems still attached

1/2 cup	sugar	125 mL
1	bottle red wine	1

Carefully peel the pears, leaving the stems attached. Turn the pears upside down and, using a narrow-bladed knife, scoop out as much of the core as you can. Trim the bottom of the pear if necessary so that it stands upright.

In a pan just large enough to hold all the pears, dissolve the sugar in the wine over low heat. Place the pears in the wine and simmer until the pears are just cooked. Leave to cool in the wine. You can do this up to three days ahead.

Remove the pears and refrigerate. Bring the wine-and-sugar mixture to a boil over medium-high heat and simmer until the mixture is reduced to a syrup. Taste and add more sugar if necessary. Let syrup cool.

Carefully pour the syrup onto a large serving plate to form a lake. Stand pears upright in the syrup. Serve at room temperature with cream or crème fraîche.

Serves 6

Bon appétit.

ACKNOWLEDGEMENTS

WITH SPECIAL THANKS to Alma Lee, and to Sally Harding and Robert Mackwood of Seventh Avenue Literary Agency. *Merci aussi* to fellow francophile Scott Steedman of Raincoast Books for the amiable edits. Above all, our thanks to all the friends named in this book who have shared their glorious region with us over the years.

PHOTO BY PHILLIP CHIN

ABOUT ANGELA MURRILLS
AND PETER MATTHEWS

ANGELA MURRILLS writes on food, wine and lifestyle for many publications, including *The Georgia Straight, Nuvo, Western Living, The National Post, The Globe and Mail* and *Food Arts.* In her ongoing pursuit of stories with the ring of truth, she has worked on the production line in a chocolate factory, learned to make roti in an Indian desert and undertaken a blind tasting of 50 Sauternes at nine o'clock in the morning. Angela is the author of *Food City: Vancouver.* She and her husband, retired art director PETER MATTHEWS, divide their time between Vancouver and the Languedoc.